Philosophical Inquiry

The *Big Ideas for Young Thinkers Book Series* brings together the results of recent research about pre-college philosophy. There has been sizable growth in philosophy programs for young people. The book series provides readers with a way to learn about all that is taking place in this important area of philosophical and educational practice. It brings together work from around the globe by some of the foremost practitioners of philosophy for children. The books in the series include single-author works as well as essay collections. With a premium placed on accessibility, the book series allows readers to discover the exciting world of pre-college philosophy.

Philosophical Inquiry

Combining the Tools of Philosophy with Inquiry-Based Teaching and Learning

Philip Cam

ROWMAN & LITTLEFIELD
Lanham • Boulder • New York • London

Published by Rowman & Littlefield
An imprint of The Rowman & Littlefield Publishing Group, Inc.
4501 Forbes Boulevard, Suite 200, Lanham, Maryland 20706
www.rowman.com

6 Tinworth Street, London SE11 5AL, United Kingdom

Copyright © 2020 by Philip Cam

All rights reserved. No part of this book may be reproduced in any form or by any electronic or mechanical means, including information storage and retrieval systems, without written permission from the publisher, except by a reviewer who may quote passages in a review.

British Library Cataloguing in Publication Information Available

Library of Congress Cataloging-in-Publication Data

Library of Congress Control Number: 2019956619

ISBN: 978-1-4758-4628-7 (cloth : alk. paper)
ISBN: 978-1-4758-4629-4 (pbk. : alk. paper)
ISBN: 978-1-4758-4630-0 (electronic)

♾️™ The paper used in this publication meets the minimum requirements of American National Standard for Information Sciences—Permanence of Paper for Printed Library Materials, ANSI/NISO Z39.48-1992.

Contents

Foreword	vii
Preface	ix
Acknowledgments	xi
Introduction	xiii

1 Getting Started ... 1
  Arranging the Classroom and Setting the Rules ... 4
  Structuring a Lesson ... 6
  A Toolkit for Thinking ... 8
  Learning Outcomes ... 13

2 Questioning ... 15
  Question Starters ... 16
  Thinking about Response Demands ... 17
  The Question Quadrant ... 20
  Factual, Evaluative, and Conceptual Questions ... 24
  Setting an Agenda ... 25
  Unpacking Problems and Questions ... 26
  The Teacher as Procedural Questioner ... 27
  The Characteristics of Philosophical Questions ... 35
  Constructing Discussion Plans ... 41
  Exercises and Activities ... 42

3 Conceptual Exploration ... 53
  Categorical Operations ... 55
  Comparative Operations ... 66
  Complex Concepts ... 70

Clarification	74
Exercises and Activities	76
4 Reasoning	**103**
The Language of Reasoning	103
Justification and Inference	105
Conditional Reasoning	108
Deductive Reasoning	111
Inductive Reasoning	122
Necessary and Sufficient Conditions	128
Contradiction and Logical Impossibility	130
Analyzing and Evaluating Reasoning	130
Mapping Arguments in Discussion	132
Exercises and Activities	136
Bibliography	157
About the Author	159

Foreword

Thomas E. Wartenberg, Series Editor

Many teachers of young children are interested in introducing their students to philosophy but feel intimidated because they have never studied it themselves. Despite reassurances that they can do it, many remain unconvinced.

After reading Philip Cam's *Philosophical Inquiry: Combining the Tools of Philosophy with Inquiry-Based Teaching and Learning* all such qualms should be eliminated. Cam's "thinking tools" approach breaks down the intimidating idea of teaching philosophy into simple units that anyone can master. The book provides teachers with everything they need to know about teaching philosophy to young children, and it does so in a very clear and easily understandable manner.

Cam divides the skills necessary for philosophizing into three broad categories: (1) questioning, (2) conceptual exploration, and (3) reasoning. Each of these is, in turn, broken down into various different subcategories, enabling a teacher and her students to take a step-by-step approach to learning how to take part in a philosophy discussion. For example, such discussions generally are initiated with a question such as "Was what Frog did fair?" But determining what types of questions count as philosophical requires some practice. Cam provides a clear series of steps for learning how to decide what questions are philosophical and which are not. He also supplies some very useful tools, such as the "question quadrant," to help both teachers and their students recognize what types of questions are philosophical ones.

Throughout the book, Cam provides exercises and illustrations of all the ideas that students need to learn so that they can have philosophical discussions with their classmates. The teacher's task is made easier because Cam provides all the materials a teacher needs to use in her classroom, so that they can easily develop the knowledge and skills they will need to be a successful philosophy teacher.

Cam has developed his thinking tools method through years of work with teachers and students in Australia and Asia. I am very excited to be able to bring his revolutionary method for teaching philosophy to a broader audience. *Philosophical Inquiry* is an important contribution to the literature on teaching philosophy in schools that will help all those who use it to develop exciting and manageable philosophy programs for their students.

Preface

Philosophical Inquiry comes from half a lifetime of working with teachers. Having started out as a school teacher before my love for philosophy eventually led me to further study and an academic career, it was from the beginning clear to me that the ways of thinking and kinds of concerns that come out of the ancient discipline of philosophy have a great deal to contribute to the education of the young. Social and economic developments over the intervening period have only strengthened this belief. More than ever, young people need the skills and abilities that can be derived from philosophy.

It is no longer sufficient, if ever it was, for education to implant reproducible subject knowledge. In order to thrive socially and economically in the world today, we need to be able to think critically, creatively, and in socially responsible ways, which means using knowledge to solve problems, deal with issues, explore possibilities and work with ideas, both individually and in collaboration with others. That this has implications for the curriculum and teaching methods is obvious. Solutions must be found.

The solution I present in this book is grounded in both theory and practice. It combines the tools of philosophy with collaborative inquiry-based teaching and learning. By extending our teaching in this way, we can strengthen students' abilities to think about what they are taught and to develop a deeper understanding of it. Students also become used to working productively together while showing care and concern for one another. This integration of cognitive and social development is by no means incidental. It is a remarkably effective way to develop both powers of thought and social abilities.

Having seen the transformation that these tools and ways of working have brought to schools and classrooms of all descriptions around the world, I have no doubt that almost any teacher can do likewise with a modicum of application. By using your own intelligence and imagination you will quickly see how to apply the tools and methods introduced in this book to your own teaching context. Perseverance will not only bring results. Like many teachers before you, it may well turn out to be one of the most rewarding ventures of your teaching career.

Acknowledgments

All of us owe much more to our teachers than we can ever repay. I had a wonderful teacher in Michael Bradley when I was an undergraduate in philosophy at the University of Adelaide and in my supervisor John Mackie when I was a graduate student at Oxford. They taught me a great deal about conceptual analysis and reasoning. Later, I became acquainted with and befriended Matthew Lipman, who developed the groundbreaking program of Philosophy for Children. To both him and his colleague, Ann Margaret Sharp, I owe a deep debt of gratitude. Through them, the educational work of John Dewey and Lev Vygotsky, which I had first read in teacher's college many years before, came to life.

I would like to thank Tom Wartenberg and Rowman & Littlefield for inviting me to contribute to the series *Big Ideas for Young Thinkers*. It has given me a further opportunity to express these ideas and bring them to a new readership. Finally, I would like to thank my wife, Heather, for her patient support while I spent the countless hours that all authors put in working away in the study.

Introduction

Philosophical Inquiry introduces teachers to a philosophical approach to collaborative inquiry-based teaching and learning. The tools of philosophy fit with this style of teaching and learning like a hand to a glove. Together, they provide a robust means of developing the ability of students to think and work with one another in ways that meet the demands of contemporary education. The book aims to provide teachers with the knowledge and understanding that will allow them to add this timely innovation to their teaching repertoire.

The "thinking tools" approach to the planning and delivery of collaborative inquiry-based lessons gives it real teeth. In addition to providing teachers with the overall approach, however, there are detailed practical introductions to the three main topics that any teacher must know about if they are to make a success of an inquiry-based approach to teaching. These topics are questioning, conceptual exploration, and reasoning.

To inquire is first and foremost to question. This means that the teacher needs to be a proficient questioner, and students should be taught to explore and probe issues and problems by becoming questioners themselves. Students must develop that art if they are to learn to inquire. While young children have a natural propensity to ask questions, there is a lot to learn about how to be an effective questioner when it comes to inquiry.

Teachers complain that students often have a poor understanding of basic concepts that they are trying to teach. More often than not, the problem is that students lack the tools for analyzing the ideas with which they have to grapple. Since philosophy specializes in conceptual analysis, it can help remedy this situation by adapting its tools of conceptual exploration for the purpose.

Outside of mathematical deduction, school education seldom pays systematic attention to reasoning. This is a serious neglect, since most of the occasions when reasoning is called for in everyday life require reasoning in language. Aside from the fact that logic—the study of reasoning—is a branch of philosophy, philosophers pay special attention to reasoning. So, this neglect is also something that the tools of philosophy can be used to redress.

Let us look at all of this chapter by chapter. Chapter 1 shows how the tools and practices being recommended meet contemporary demands for critical thinking skills, problem-solving abilities, and a capacity to innovate and work with ideas. It provides practical advice for setting up a classroom and structuring lessons for this kind of work, and teachers are introduced to a basic kit of tools that students will need in order to carry it out. It also provides a detailed list of the kinds of intellectual and social skills and abilities that this work develops.

Chapter 2 takes up the topic of questioning. Teachers are shown how to use question starters for the purposes of inquiry and alerted to the response demands of various kinds of questions. The chapter introduces ways of teaching students to recognize questions that call for inquiry and of developing their ability to construct, unpack, and get questions in order. It also contains a detailed account of the role of the teacher as questioner in facilitating inquiry-based learning and shows how to make use of questions in planning lessons.

Chapter 3 deals with conceptual exploration. It shows how to teach basic conceptual operations. This includes categorical operations, such as those of classification and division, conceptual opposition, distinction-making and definition, as well as the comparative operations involved in ordinal comparison and comparisons of quality and quantity. The chapter also shows how to explore complex concepts and uncover the criteria that govern them. It ends with ways of attending to vagueness and ambiguity that help students to express their thoughts more clearly.

Chapter 4 brings us to reasoning. It begins with the language students use in reasoning and the basic operations of justification and inference. It acknowledges and makes use of the widespread use of conditional ("if . . . then") reasoning, but also introduces the basic forms of both deductive and inductive reasoning. Teachers are shown how to teach students to reconstruct and evaluate arguments that are put to them as well as to avoid fundamental errors and to reason proficiently. The chapter also shows you how to map reasoning in discussion.

Exercises and activities are used for illustration throughout the book in order to make each topic clear in a practical way. In addition, the chapters on questioning, conceptual exploration, and reasoning all end with a rich array of exercises and activities. They provide elementary, middle school, and secondary teachers with materials on all sorts of subjects with which they can make a start in the classroom.

Chapter 1

Getting Started

> All which the school can or need do for pupils, so far as their *minds* are concerned . . . is to develop their ability to think.
>
> John Dewey

We hear a great deal these days about the need to educate students for the twenty-first century. It is a recognition of the fact that traditional content-based education is no longer sufficient for young people to be able to make the most of their opportunities in a world of rapid technological, economic, and social change. Without some adjustment, that older style of education will no longer fit them for the world in which they are growing up, let alone the one coming over the horizon.

While the focus of such remarks is often on digital literacy, that is only one ingredient in the mix of skills, abilities and dispositions to which attention has been drawn. Critical thinking skills and problem-solving abilities are stressed, as is the ability to be innovative and to work with ideas. Adaptability is also key. This includes being self-directed as the occasion demands but also a good collaborator when required. It means being able to effectively communicate your own ideas while also prepared to engage positively with other people's suggestions.

Aside from keeping abreast of technology, it is a remarkable fact that many of these twenty-first-century attributes have been exhibited by the best thinkers throughout human history. Anyone who has read the dialogues of Plato, or poured over the notebooks of Leonardo da Vinci, will have seen many of them exhibited there.

Plato's inquiries into concepts such as friendship, virtue, knowledge, and beauty exhibit masterly analytical skill with complex ideas, while providing a model of reasonableness in the exploration of different possibilities and viewpoints. Leonardo's notebooks are a tour de force of intelligent observation, exploration, invention, and problem-solving.

These examples could be endlessly multiplied, making it clear that educators are not being asked to attend to newly minted skills and abilities, so much as to nurture aptitudes that have been there all along. Not everyone can be a Plato or a Leonardo, of course, but that is not the point. It is rather that the kinds of capacities they exhibited in outstanding ways are ones that all of us are capable of developing to some degree, and education is being called upon to place far more emphasis upon them than it has to date.

The skills being talked about include what are sometimes called "soft skills" involved in such things as critical thinking and problem-solving, creativity, and communication. To call these skills "soft" may give the impression that they lack hard muscle or rigor, unlike the traditional skills of numeracy and literacy. That would be a mistake. Critical thinking and problem-solving can display great strength, as well as precision and attention to detail. Creative thinking requires concentration, powers of invention, and vigor. Communication of complex ideas requires skills of a higher order than those of basic arithmetic, spelling, and grammar.

So-called soft skills and abilities are also sometimes thought of as subjective and hard to quantify, and therefore not readily able to be taught or assessed. In truth, there is nothing particularly subjective about having poor communication skills, lack of imagination, or failing to think critically. Deficiencies of these kinds lie at the low end of the scale of performances that are readily recognizable and gradable by those who know what they are doing.

Similar remarks apply to teaching such things. Nothing much can be taught by those who have little idea how to do so, of course, but that only points to the need for appropriate teaching methods.

It is clear that the educational transformation being called for has widespread and systemic consequences for the curriculum as well as teaching methods. Different areas of the curriculum naturally adapt to change in their own way, of course, but this needs to occur within a general framework that maintains the overall integrity of educational change. We therefore need to focus on general features rather than subject-specific ones.

As with the glance at great thinkers of the past, stepping back in time provides a clue to what is needed. From an historical perspective, nearly all the specialized disciplines that underlie the curriculum branched off from the parent discipline of philosophy at one time or another. In the ancient world, scientific speculation and mathematics, as well as ethics and social thought were all branches of philosophy.

Between them, Plato and Aristotle covered pretty much every field, from the foundations of knowledge and existence to logic, the natural world, society, and ethics. Even at the start of the modern period the natural sciences were conceived of as natural philosophy, while the social sciences branched off from philosophy long after that.

All of these areas of inquiry retain underground connections with philosophy. When stripped of their technical trappings and specialized methods, their philosophical groundings are often revealed. For example, Einstein wrote a little book to explain relativity theory to the reader who has nothing more than secondary school mathematics.[1] There is in fact very little math in the book and much of it involves thought experiments that help the reader to reconceive the basic framework for understanding the notions of space, time, energy, and matter. Most of it could pass for the work of a philosopher.

Over its long history, philosophy has developed a wide range of general-purpose tools for carrying out intellectual work. These center on problem-formation, questioning, the construction and analysis of hypotheses and theories, and reasoning about them. While modern disciplines broke away from philosophy as they developed their specialized methods, they have never entirely dispensed with these ways of working. Equally, contemporary philosophers can be found digging into the foundations of all the disciplines, whether in the philosophy of science and mathematics, historical and social studies, or the study of literature and art.

This means that philosophy stands in a special relationship to the specialized disciplines. It has a wide-ranging interest in the subject matter of the other disciplines and they have inherited thinking tools from philosophy that remain indispensable. Philosophy is therefore in a unique position when we are looking for general-purpose skills and abilities with deep connections to the various areas of study.

In fact, when we begin to examine this array in more detail, these skills and abilities look like they were taken straight from a manual of basic philosophical thinking practices: analysis of concepts, reasoning, reflecting, identifying alternative possibilities, generating ideas, and problem-solving.

In addition to cognitive capabilities, it is also important to acknowledge those that have a more obviously social character. These include being able to effectively communicate ideas, willingness to acknowledge other people's perspectives, and being adaptable and open-minded. These traits are by no means the exclusive preserve of philosophy, but it is worth noting how well they comport with it.

Philosophy is an exploration of ideas that employs the tools required for clear and orderly expression and communication. It involves a contest of ideas that encourages the careful consideration of others' suggestions. It makes those who engage in it less dogmatic and more willing to change their minds in response to good reasons and evidence.

While schools have tended to treat students as cognitive beings in relation to their studies and as social beings regarding their other conduct, the cognitive and social aspects of education that are now coming into play need to work together. Combination of the cognitive and social is indeed the hallmark of the capabilities in question.

To discuss ideas, for instance, involves engaging with other people. It includes giving them reasons for what you think and actively considering what they say. It means building on their contributions as well as effectively communicating your own ideas. The same applies to learning to deal with disagreement. Being reasonable in our dealings with other people is grounded in our preparedness to engage with them in the give-and-take of reasons.

We may sum up these introductory remarks by restating the relationship between the ends to be achieved and the proposed means of doing so. The basic idea is to engage students in collaborative inquiry-based learning that employs tools and ways of working derived from philosophy to meet the demand for the outcomes in school education that are being pressed upon us. We are going back to the ancient discipline of philosophy to equip students with the capacities that they will need in this rapidly changing world.

ARRANGING THE CLASSROOM AND SETTING THE RULES

Let us start by considering a basic classroom setup. Collaborative learning requires that students are able to communicate effectively with one another. While that can mean communication in writing or through the intermediary of electronic devices, these are not the basic forms of communication. It starts with face-to-face interaction. In the classroom, that may mean students working as a whole class as well as in pairs and small groups. A mixture of all three groupings is generally desirable and which of them is appropriate at a given moment depends upon the task at hand.

This acknowledges the leading role of speaking and listening in collaborative learning. To focus on the capacities that we are trying to develop, we need to put speaking and listening ahead of reading and writing. Skills that are first introduced by the teacher in discursive activities with the class can be gradually bedded down in discussion between peers. Once students have internalized them in this way, they are ready to employ them in written work.

Since whole class discussion facilitated by the teacher is the entry point, let us begin with that. The first thing to note is that effective class discussion requires an appropriate physical setup. We are talking about face-to-face verbal communication and that requires the participants to face one another. In order that each member of the class can see the face of every other member, you ideally need to form the class into a circle. Young students may be seated on the floor, but otherwise a circle of chairs is best. Unless desks are absolutely necessary for what you intend to do, they can be dispensed with for this kind of activity.

Class discussion needs to be orderly. Otherwise the interlocking cognitive and social capabilities that it is designed to develop will not materialize. Here are some basic points that students need to keep in mind:

- Only one person is to speak at a time. This includes students not talking over the top of one another or indulging in private conversations while someone else is speaking. In the elementary and junior secondary school, it is a good idea to use a speaker's ball—a basketball, say, that can be rolled across the floor. If you have the ball, then you are the speaker. Otherwise you are a listener.
- Students should avoid the habit of constantly addressing the teacher rather than their peers. This ingrained habit can be hard to break. It is important to do so, however, as collaborative learning depends upon students communicating directly with one another.
- Some students need to remember to give other people a chance to speak. While talkative students can be an asset in the early stages, they should not be allowed to monopolize discussion. If a small group of students come to dominate the class, it will deprive other students of learning opportunities.
- Don't allow students to have their hands up while someone is speaking. It can mean that they are thinking about what they want to say and not actively listening to others and can be off-putting for the current speaker. If you use a speaker's ball, you can have speakers indicate that they are finishing off by having them place their hands on the top of the ball. Then hands can go up.
- A discussion is not a series of disconnected utterances. It needs to make progress. This means that contributing to discussion is not just a matter of having your say regardless of its relevance. Students should try to build upon one another's ideas.
- Any substantial discussion is likely to give voice to different opinions and ideas. There is a difference, however, between expressing your disagreement with what someone has said and attacking them. A simple way of making the point is to say that there should be no put-downs.
- An inquiry is an exploration of ideas in a search for truth or meaning. While it involves a contest of ideas, it is collaborative and not about winning an

argument. It also means being prepared to change your mind on the basis of reason and evidence.

It is essential for students to have discussion rules, regardless of how you introduce them. A simple set goes as follows:

- Only one person is to speak at a time.
- Pay attention to the person who is speaking.
- Speak to other students rather than to the teacher.
- Give other people a chance to speak.
- Build upon other people's ideas.
- No put-downs.

There are various ways to help make discussion rules effective. You can explore their importance with the class. You can make the rules visible by displaying them. You can engage in direct intervention when breaches occur. A little further down the track, you can even hand over the task of maintaining compliance to responsible students. For example, you can give a card that reads "Only one person is to speak at a time" to a dependable student, which they can hold up in the air if there is an infringement.

STRUCTURING A LESSON

While collaborative inquiry-based teaching and learning can take many forms, it is best to begin with a basic or "plain vanilla" lesson structure. That makes it easier to vary the design while retaining its essential features. The basic lesson plan goes as follows:

Begin with a Warm-up

This is a brief exercise or activity to prepare students for the lesson. It can include such things as introducing a thinking tool that will be employed in the lesson, carrying out a related exercise, allowing for quick responses to find out what students understand about the topic or issue in hand, or having students recapitulate the findings of the previous lesson.

Introduce a Stimulus and Raise Questions

A suitable stimulus is needed to arouse thoughtful interest in the topic or issue to be discussed. This is followed by having students raise questions or problems, clarifying them, knocking them into shape, and then choosing the most important or promising question or group of questions to pursue.

Guide Discussion

Initiate discussion using the selected students' questions and assist the class to examine the matter systematically. Discussion needs to be guided by the rules mentioned earlier, and the teacher should prompt students to make appropriate moves in their thinking when necessary, ensuring that discussion moves forward in an orderly and productive way. This can be assisted by the gradual introduction of the thinking tools that are listed in the following section.

Introduce Activities or Exercises

An activity may be introduced at an appropriate point to give greater depth to the discussion of an issue, problem, or concept. Alternatively, a content-related exercise may be introduced to focus attention on a skill and give students practice. Both activities and exercises normally involve at least some small group work or work in pairs.

Provide Closure

Closure is usually best achieved by way of reflection on the work carried out. It may involve student evaluation of the progress made in addressing the matter under discussion or having students assess one or more aspects of their social and intellectual conduct. Brief discussion is generally desirable. Having students discuss their performance helps them to become more responsible for its improvement.

We can see what a plain vanilla lesson looks like in practice by glancing over a lesson planner. Notice that the skill base of the lesson has been distinguished from the content learning outcomes. This makes it clear that the focus is on developing the capacity of students to think and cooperate, in addition to acquiring knowledge of the subject matter. It recognizes that collaborative inquiry is a vital means of acquiring knowledge of subject matter.

When carried out effectively, the process outlined above is a prescription for robust and rigorous classroom inquiry in which students learn to probe problems and issues through questioning, constructing, analyzing and testing their thoughts, and reasoning with them proficiently. It takes time and effort on the part of both teachers and students to master the process, but the benefits to be derived will more than repay the effort.

Class:	Date:	Number of students:
Statement of content learning outcomes:		
Focus inquiry skills/abilities:	Focus social skills/abilities:	

Duration	Lesson	Resources
	Warm-up:	
	Stimulus for the lesson:	
	Discussion plan:	
	Activity or exercise:	
	Closure/Reflection:	

A TOOLKIT FOR THINKING

In order to successfully examine an issue or a problem, we need to be able to size it up and ask the right questions. We need a source of ideas, possibilities, hypotheses, or other suggestions by way of tentative answers. We need to examine these suggestions in the light of reason and evidence. Along the way, we need to search for useful connections, make appropriate distinctions, and employ suitable criteria to guide our judgments. The best way to train students to do these things is to teach them to use the associated tools.

Much like learning a trade, students need to be taught how to think things through by inquiring into them. Tradespeople would be worse than useless if they turned up to a job without the necessary tools, or if they had the tools but lacked proficiency in their use. Much the same applies here. Unless students are familiar with the tools they need and know how to use them, they cannot be expected to do a good job. Just like the trainee electrician or auto mechanic, they need to be instructed in the tools of their trade and given practice in their use.

The following is a list of basic tools for inquiry that should be gradually introduced and then used when it is appropriate.

Questions

Students need to learn to ask open questions when probing into problems and issues. As the old saying goes, the right question asked is often half the problem solved. By the same token, students who do not know how to put their finger on what needs to be questioned, or are not even in the habit of asking questions, will be stymied from the start. The art of asking needful questions is an essential tool in the inquirer's kit.

In collaborative inquiry, students learn to raise questions not only in relation to subject matter. They also become skilled at questioning one another. When they are trying to become clear about what someone is saying, are attempting to follow its implications, or trying to find out why someone thinks what they do, they ask each other appropriate questions. An inquirer is a questioner and students learn to work together in this way throughout their inquiries.

Suggestions

Questions that delve into live problems and issues are unlike those that teachers ask when they expect students to know the answer. Nor are they likely to be ones where students can simply look up the answer. Rather, they are far more likely to call upon students to use their subject knowledge in order to express their thoughts or ideas. To express your thoughts on the matter, or to put an idea forward in the hope that it may be useful, is to make a suggestion rather than to provide the answer. Even to have a stab at an answer is to engage in a quite different kind of process than answering the questions that teachers typically ask.

Attempts to answer the questions that set the agenda for inquiry involve divergence of thought. They do not follow the linear pattern of thinking associated with such things as answering a question by repeating information that has been taught or working out the right answer to a "problem" in math through the application of an algorithm. Fanning out to search for possibilities and welcoming different ideas or opinions is an indispensable part of the process.

To offer your opinion, admit a possibility, or speculate as to what may be the case is not to say what you know to be right or true. It is to suggest something that may turn out to be so upon further investigation. Even when they are not much more than a guess, these suggestions are not idle. In idle speculation we are not really interested in exploring the merits of our conjectures, whereas the opposite is true in inquiry. Inquiry proceeds by putting them to the test.

Reasons

The examination of suggestions through the give-and-take of reasons is a prominent feature of collaborative classroom inquiry. It is not just that the teacher may ask students to give reasons for what they say. They come to expect this of one another. If little is to be said for a suggestion, or there is an abundance of contrary evidence, it won't survive long. It will also not win through if it doesn't stack up against competing suggestions.

Reasons are of various sorts. To identify the reason why something happened is to *explain* its occurrence. People also give reasons for what they do in order to *justify* their actions. The giving of reasons to explain and justify is common and familiar. In collaborative inquiry, however, we are particularly concerned to give and consider reasons for what we put forward. Reasons may be given to back up a claim, give some credence to a suggestion, or to show that a contrary proposition is more likely to be true. This use of reasons is called "logical justification."

Examples

It is often appropriate for students to provide examples in their inquiries. They can show that things are at least sometimes as they say by providing an example. A more sweeping statement increases its plausibility when it is borne out in a variety of cases. Examples can also serve as illustrations, as when concrete examples are used to explain an abstract idea, helping the class to gain a greater appreciation of what it involves.

One use of examples deserves special mention. A single contrary example is sufficient to show that an unqualified generalization is false. Students who leap to the conclusion that things are always thus or never so, or who engage in stereotypical remarks and other unwarranted generalizations, can find themselves having to retract or modify what they say when other students offer what is called a "counterexample"—an example, that is to say, which runs counter to their claim.

Classification and Division

Classification and division are basic conceptual operations that do a great deal of work. To classify things is simply to assign them to a more general class. Division is the reverse operation of dividing things of some kind into various subclasses. These operations are as elementary and important in learning to think conceptually as are addition and subtraction in learning to think mathematically. Familiarity with them enables students to manipulate ideas and brings precision and order to the conceptual side of their thought.

These operations are pervasive. An example identifies something as a thing of some kind. Coherent division into subclasses enables us to bring order to things as diverse as biological species and supermarket shelves. Distinction-making depends upon arriving at an appropriate division between things that belong to the same more general kind. Even traditional definition is a combination of classification and division. To say that a cavalcade is a procession on horseback, for example, is to classify it as a procession that is different from processions of other kinds by being on horseback. This is all part of conceptual proficiency.

Criteria

It is one thing to make a judgment and another to be able to state the basis on which it was made. Knowing the basis of a judgment enables us to hold that judgment to account. Good judgments employ appropriate criteria. Judgments lacking in this regard are likely to be poor. They may be poor because they rely on inappropriate criteria or because they lack any clear basis at all. We have much to gain, therefore, by being attentive to the criteria on which we base our judgments. One way of developing this awareness in students is to have them examine the criteria on which they rely in making their judgments.

The criteria that govern the application of a concept are especially of interest in classroom inquiry. If students judge that something isn't fair, for instance, an examination of their reasons for saying so will reveal the criteria they rely upon to make that judgment. Whether the judgment can be sustained when the criteria upon which it is based are scrutinized is something that only careful consideration can reveal.

Socially significant concepts like fairness are almost always complex in the sense that a variety of criteria may be applicable and those criteria may weigh differently in different situations. This is often a source of conflicting judgments, in this case as to whether something is fair or not. It is in the nature of such things that thoughtful people do not always agree about them even when they examine them carefully. Exploring these disagreements provides students with a deeper understanding of important concepts, however, and teaches them to be reasonable in dealing with disagreement.

Thought Experiments

It is often useful to test our ideas against imagined situations or scenarios to see how they fare. The same applies to critiquing other people's suggestions. This is known as a thought experiment. Here is an example from the philosopher Robert Nozick.[2] In challenging the suggestion that we should always act so as to maximize our pleasure, he asks us to imagine being permanently plugged into an "experience machine" that would supply us with endless pleasure, regardless of what happened in our lives. If pleasure were the only good, we shouldn't hesitate. Nozick is betting that we would.

Students can use these "What if . . ." or "Suppose that . . ." scenarios to examine ideas, issues, and problems through imagined possibilities. It is a productive way of combining critical thinking with imagination. It reminds us that, far from being opposed to one another, critical and creative thinking can work together productively in dealing with problems and issues. As was mentioned in Einstein's case, thought experiments can combine critical and creative thinking of a very high order.

Inferences

Just as we may make an assertion and then state reasons to justify it, we may treat those statements as premises from which to infer that assertion as conclusion. Students are more familiar with giving reasons than with drawing inferences, with the exception of mathematics, which depends heavily on inference-making. They cannot be proficient in reasoning about issues and ideas, however, without being able to move between them with ease. The two operations may be introduced independently, but students should be made aware of their connection before too long and given practice in moving from reason-giving to inference-making and vice versa.

Students need to learn to become familiar with two types of inferences: deductive inferences and inductive ones. In a deductive inference, the conclusion follows from what are called its premises with logical certainty. If the premises are true, the conclusion is guaranteed to be true—as long as there are no mistakes in our reasoning. Think of doing simple arithmetic, or constructing a geometrical proof, and you'll get the idea.

Inductive inferences do not provide this guarantee. The premises give us merely some reason to suppose that the conclusion is true. As with arguments presented in court, they may add to its likelihood, or even make it a practical certainty, but logically speaking it is always possible for the premises to be true while the conclusion is false.

The tools of inquiry need to be explicitly introduced and exercised, as well as built into inquiry-based tasks. Every inquiry-based lesson should incorporate a focus thinking tool or two and students should know that they are expected to use them. Students are far more likely to make good use of their tools when that aspect of a task is made highly visible. Here is a list of suggestions for increasing the visibility of the tools that they need to do their work:

- For younger students, especially in the early stages, associate each tool with a logo and have the focus tool or tools for the lesson on display.
- Have a wall chart displaying the tools permanently up in the classroom.
- Employ skill-building exercises dedicated to use of a tool (such as those to be found at the end of the subsequent chapters of this book) and display some of this work in the classroom.

- Emphasize the use of the language associated with the tools, as in "John has given us a *reason* for thinking that Sarah is right. What do others think?" and "Can anyone think of a *counterexample*?"
- Ask students to emphasize the tools that they are using in their offerings too. For example, a student might say, "I think that that Sarah is right for the following *reason*" or "I have a *counterexample* to what John just said."
- Have students afterward identify the tools that they used (or should have used) in an activity.
- Occasionally divide the class in two and use a fishbowl technique where the outer circle has a checklist of the tools and keeps track of their use in a discussion conducted by students in the inner circle.
- Have a worksheet where students can keep track of their own tool usage and the development of their proficiency.

LEARNING OUTCOMES

Earlier we distinguished between the content learning outcomes and the skill base of a lesson. The content learning outcomes relate to the subject matter, whereas the skill base refers to the specific skills to which attention is to be paid during the lesson. As you become familiar with the contents of this book, you will gain a more detailed knowledge of the skills and abilities that collaborative classroom inquiry promotes.

Still, by way of conclusion to this chapter, it is worth looking at an indicative list of skills, to get an impression of what lies ahead. Each lesson should have both an inquiry and a collaborative focus, but needs to be restricted to one or two skills of each kind.

Inquiry Skills and Abilities

- Formulating inquiry questions
- Making suggestions
- Clarifying
- Justifying
- Explaining
- Identifying alternative possibilities
- Weighing reasons and evidence
- Making distinctions
- Defining
- Classifying
- Identifying differences of kind
- Identifying differences of degree

- Formulating and applying criteria
- Using examples
- Using counterexamples
- Constructing thought experiments
- Using conditional reasoning
- Making deductive inferences
- Making inductive inferences
- Identifying premises
- Identifying assumptions
- Identifying conclusions
- Constructing and evaluating arguments

Social Skills and Abilities

- Actively listening
- Contributing to discussion
- Taking your turn
- Allowing others to have their say
- Acknowledging others' contributions
- Building on others' contributions
- Inviting others' contributions
- Assisting others to make inquiry moves
- Showing respect for others' viewpoints
- Helping to evaluate others' contributions
- Engaging in dialogue
- Engaging in the give-and-take of reasons
- Exploring disagreement respectfully
- Conceding mistakes
- Acknowledging a change of mind
- Asking procedural questions
- Helping to synthesize suggestions
- Working effectively with a partner
- Playing an assigned role in a small group
- Playing an assigned role in class discussion

NOTES

1. Albert Einstein, *Relativity: The Special and the General Theory* (New York: Bonanza Books, 1961).

2. See Robert Nozick, *Anarchy, State and Utopia* (New York: Basic Books, 1974), 42–45.

Chapter 2

Questioning

A prudent question is one-half of wisdom.

Francis Bacon

To inquire is first and foremost to question. Questions arise when we begin to wonder about things, become curious as to what they mean, or why they are so. They come to mind when things do not turn out as we expected or are uncertain how to proceed. They urge themselves upon us when we want to know the truth.

In all such cases, we realize that something eludes our grasp—something we gesture toward, or try to put our finger on, by asking questions. We need to address them if we are to satisfy our curiosity, explain our predicament, relieve our uncertainty, or overcome our ignorance. Such questions provide a starting point for inquiry.

Children are naturally inquisitive and their curiosity gives rise to questioning. There comes a stage when they may irritate their parents by pestering them with questions. Parents may be forgiven for not knowing how to turn this inclination to good account, but the same cannot be said for school education. Education should nurture children's natural curiosity and build upon it. This requires a sustained effort that is too seldom made, leaving what could become one of the great fruits of learning to wither on the vine.

While children are active questioners long before they come to school, it does not mean they can readily formulate appropriate questions in educational contexts. They have to learn how to ask questions that point them in the right direction when it comes to inquiring into subject matter in the classroom. As with any other general ability that we cultivate in school, it requires systematic guidance and the kind of sustained effort that is provided by inquiry-based teaching and learning.

QUESTION STARTERS

As early childhood educators know, students need to be taught about the form that questions take. This includes using common question starters, such as "what," "where," "when," "how," "who," and "why," as well as to identify questions with inflection in speech and question marks in writing. For the purposes of inquiry, we need to add words such as "could" and "might," given that an inquiry is an investigation into possibilities: different lines of inquiry that need to be pursued. We also need words like "ought" and "should" to raise questions about values and conduct, which is a socially significant area of classroom inquiry.

It is worth noting the importance of "Why?" as a basic question starter in inquiry-based learning. "Why-questions" call for a reason and the giving and examination of reasons is an essential part of the inquiry process. "Why-questions" can be divided into those that seek an explanation and those that ask for a justification. Among justifications, we also need to distinguish between reasons aimed at justifying an action or some state-of-affairs and those that attempt to justify a proposition or claim. The latter is the bread and butter of collaborative inquiry.

Here are a couple of question starter activities for the early years that can be used as preliminaries to inquiry. The second one is more advanced than the first.

Activity: Questions and Statements

1. Write a mixture of statements and questions, such as the ones below, on strips of card.
   - Who has a question?
   - I have a question.
   - What do you like to think about?
   - I like to think about my friends.
   - I am thinking about my fluffy black kitten.
   - What is its name?
2. Form the class into a circle and place the cards face down on your lap.
3. Tell the students that you are going to read a sentence and that they are to stand up if they think it is a question. If they think it is not a question, then they are to remain seated.
4. Hold up the sentence as you read it. After you read each sentence and the students have responded, read it again and place it in the center of the circle, forming two groups, one for questions and the other for statements.
5. End the activity by asking students how they can tell which sentences on the floor are questions, adding to the discussion as need be.

Activity: I Can Ask a Question

1. Write question starter words on cards and place them in a bag so that they cannot be seen.
2. Read a story from a picture book. Something short and simple is best.
3. Ask a student to reach into the bag for a card and hold it up.
4. Give the class a moment to try to think of a question about the story beginning with that word that would be interesting to discuss. Then have the student holding the card select a volunteer to offer their question.
5. Write it on the board for everyone to see. Then proceed to do the same for the other question starters.
6. Choose the most interesting question for discussion.

THINKING ABOUT RESPONSE DEMANDS

When it comes to collaborative inquiry, the list of the questioning abilities that we need to teach includes

- being able to identify different kinds of questions—including, in particular, being able to distinguish a question that calls for inquiry from questions that require a different kind of response.
- being able to articulate the questions that need to be raised in their inquiries.
- being able to ask other students appropriate questions in discussing issues and ideas.
- the ability to ask yourself the right questions when thinking things through.

Let us see what these teaching outcomes involve and how we can begin to take practical steps to achieve them.

It is one thing for students to answer questions put to them by their teacher and quite another for them to ask their own questions when addressing some problem or issue. In order to develop that art, it is useful for students to become familiar with the different purposes that questions serve. It helps them to develop a feel for the kinds of questions that call for inquiry and to learn to distinguish them from questions that require a different kind of response.

The most familiar questions in teaching are those used to test knowledge or understanding. Questions used as tests of *knowledge* range from a question requiring a "Yes" or "No" answer through to statements of the relevant fact and on to more elaborate acts of recall and replication.

This is distinct from questions that test *understanding*, as when a teacher asks a question to see whether students have grasped the meaning of what they have read. This is a test of understanding because reading comprehension focuses upon the interpretation of the text, rather than simply recall of content, upon which classroom tests of knowledge principally rely.

In addition to using questions to test knowledge and understanding of material that has been taught, teachers set students' questions where they are asked to find out the answers for themselves. These are sometimes called "research" questions. The use of this term is something of a misnomer and shouldn't be equated with research in the sense of inquiry. They involve searching for and selecting information. In some cases, the task is as simple as looking up the answer in a reliable source, but it can also require students to select and arrange such material in a variety of ways.

So far, we have been dealing with what are often called "closed" questions, which are well known to teachers. These questions have established right answers and depend on such things as recollection, selection or compilation of facts, unproblematic inferences, or routine procedures. They are distinct from the "open" questions that are the lifeblood of inquiry-based teaching and learning. Open questions do not have established right answers. They often allow for a variety of answers, each with their own merits and shortcomings. Sometimes they do admit of a unique right answer, but only inquiry can reveal it.

It is important to note that open questions do not always call for inquiry. Sometimes any intelligible answer will do, or the more answers the merrier. To what uses can you put a rubber band? That's an open question and any number of answers may be given, depending upon the context, one's real-world knowledge, perseverance, and imagination.

Open questions can also admit of a variety of answers where it would be churlish or otherwise inappropriate to object to an answer that differed from one's own. Questions that go to personal tastes provide obvious examples.

The point is that these kinds of open questions do not call for answers that compete for justification by appeal to reasons and evidence—which is the very feature that characterizes the questions that demand inquiry. In inquiry, reasons or evidence will need to be given for whatever answer is offered, including reasons as to why we should endorse that answer and not another one. No matter whether we are engaged in scientific, mathematical, historical, social, or philosophical inquiry, this basic feature pertains.

A simple way to distinguish between these different kinds of questions is to ask what you would need to do in order to answer them when you don't know the answer. For example, if you need to reread a passage in order to find the answer, then that is a closed question. If it is a matter of general knowledge that you can look up, that's a closed question. If the question calls for "brainstorming" or the exercise of imagination, then it is an open question. Even so, it isn't an inquiry question if nothing more is required. It is only when answers need to be supported by reason and evidence, and weighed against competing claims, that a question calls for inquiry.

With a little effort, it is possible to teach students to reliably distinguish between these different kinds of questions by the middle elementary school years. Students must be able to do so if they are to become fully fledged inquirers. So long as the teacher asks all the questions, students are not able to really get off the ground. Unless they can distinguish one kind of question from another, they may attempt to engage in inquiry with questions that do not lend themselves to it. Nothing is more frustrating and futile. Let's start off with a couple of elementary exercises that encourage students to be mindful of what an answer requires.

Exercise: Look It Up or Work It Out?

What do you need to do to answer the following questions? Look up the answer or work it out for yourself? Circle the appropriate answer.

1. What is a dilly bag? *Look it up. Work it out.*
2. What could you do to help people in the poorest parts of Africa? *Look it up. Work it out.*
3. How many countries are there in Africa? *Look it up. Work it out.*
4. What should you do to look after a hedgehog? *Look it up. Work it out.*
5. What should you do if you have an argument with a friend? *Look it up. Work it out.*

Exercise: When Do You Need to Justify Your Answer?

Sometimes you can answer a question to suit yourself, without needing to defend what you say. On other occasions, you need to be able to justify your answer—and maybe even explain why other answers are wrong, or not as good. Which of the following questions allow you to give whatever answer you like and for which do you need to justify your answer?

1. Do you like pizza?
2. Are burgers better for you than pizza?
3. Can you have two best friends?
4. Is red your favorite color?
5. For what might you use an old tin can?
6. Is it OK sometimes to tell a lie?

Note to the teacher: You can make up your own questions for these exercises and afterward have students vote on which question would be the most interesting to discuss and then use it to hold a discussion.

THE QUESTION QUADRANT

The Question Quadrant is a tried and tested device for learning to distinguish between different kinds of questions in the classroom. In particular, it helps students to learn to distinguish inquiry questions from questions that call for a different kind of response. While there are various ways of labeling the quadrant, let's look at one that we can take as standard. It regards questions as either "open" or "closed" and as calling for either a quick response or more extensive research.

The Question Quadrant

	QUICK-ANSWER QUESTIONS		
CLOSED QUESTIONS "Look-up" answers	"Look-and-see" Questions	"Pick-and-choose" Questions	OPEN QUESTIONS "Think-up" answers
	"Extended search" Questions	Inquiry Questions	
	RESEARCH QUESTIONS		

Closed questions have settled answers. If students don't know the answer to the question, they need to turn to an appropriate source. In some cases that might mean asking the teacher, but in an independent learning task, they need to look up the answer for themselves. Some cases involve just a quick "look-and-see"—in a textbook, for instance. Others may require more complex retrieval, such as an extended Google search. In all such cases, however, we can think of these questions as having "look-up" answers.

Open questions do not have settled answers. Even if a range of informed opinion needs to be consulted, students will need to do at least a modicum of thinking for themselves if they seriously attempt to answer such questions. Once again, questions of this kind can call for a quick response where students are free to choose their answer for whatever reasons most appeal to them. In other cases, however, they are not free to simply pick-and-choose to suit themselves. They need to consider the relevant facts, explore various possibilities or points of view, and try to determine the matter as objectively as possible. These cases call for inquiry.

The Question Quadrant can be introduced from the middle elementary school years. While you may need to vary the words that you use to suit the particular year level, the following exercise shows how you can do so using simple picture books for the youngest age group.

Activity: Questions about *The Very Hungry Caterpillar*[1]

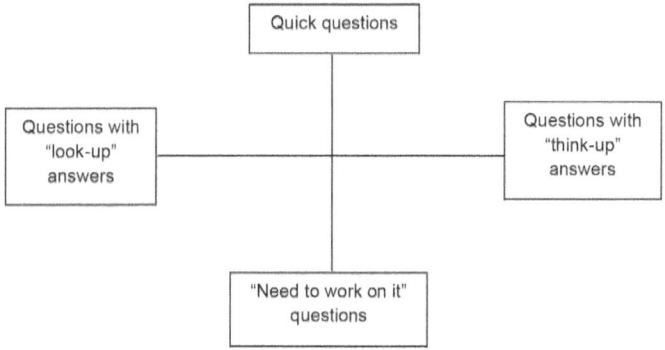

- What hatched out of the egg one sunny Sunday morning?
- What did the very hungry caterpillar eat on Monday morning?
- How do caterpillars go about making their cocoons?
- How does a caterpillar turn into a butterfly?
- What might the hungry caterpillar do when he wasn't eating?
- What else could the caterpillar have eaten besides the things mentioned in the book?
- Was the caterpillar the same living creature as the butterfly?
- Will you be the same person as you are now when you grow up to be an adult?

Procedure

1. Lay the Question Quadrant on the floor of the discussion circle, explaining it as you go with a simple example or two.

2. Read Eric Carle's *The Very Hungry Caterpillar* to the class. (Make sure that students have time to look at the pictures.)
3. Divide the class into groups and give each group a question in large print on a strip of paper.
4. Give the groups a minute or two to discuss where to place their question on the floor.
5. Have each group, in turn, place their question where they think it belongs, discussing any disagreements or uncertainty.
6. Vote on which of the inquiry questions the class would prefer to discuss and hold a discussion.

The following activity is suitable for the later elementary and junior secondary years.

Activity: The Question Quadrant

1. Construct two questions for each of the four kinds in the Question Quadrant in relation to a chosen stimulus material. Type them up in no particular order, together with a depiction of the Question Quadrant, and make sufficient copies to distribute one to each group of four students into which you will divide the class.
2. Divide the students into groups of four, provide each group with the worksheet, and explain the Question Quadrant to the class.
3. Give students a few minutes to decide where each question belongs on the Question Quadrant.
4. Take each question in turn and ask a group where it belongs on the Question Quadrant. Ask the group to justify its decision and have the class discuss any doubts or disagreements.
5. Have each group develop their own inquiry question and come out and write them up on the board.
6. Have the class critique and improve them where appropriate.
7. Take what the class regards as the most interesting question and hold a discussion, if time permits. If not, hold it over to a subsequent lesson.

Once older students are familiar with the Question Quadrant, you can reinforce it in a subsequent lesson or two by means of a worksheet. The illustration shows an example of a Question Quadrant worksheet for twelve-year-olds, based on a short article about the use and abuse of animals. The worksheet contains questions of all four types to be found in the Question Quadrant, varying the descriptors for the question categories to suit the age group, as well as to reflect the means by which the questions need to be answered. Worksheets of this kind can easily be constructed for all sorts of subject matter.

Exercise: A Right to Exploit?

Tick the appropriate column to show where the following questions belong on the Question Quadrant.

	Look-and-see	Google it	Brainstorm	Inquiry
Who was Mark Twain?				
What did Aristotle say about the relationship between plants, animals, and people?				
Why might someone keep an animal for a pet?				
Should people and animals have an equal right to life?				
Why did Immanuel Kant believe that animals cannot have the same rights as people?				
In what other ways besides those given in the text might animals be portrayed as "little people" in children's books?				
Besides oxen and horses, did ancient people use other animals for work?				
Is the fact that animals can suffer the most important thing to take into consideration in our treatment of them?				

While our interest is primarily in inquiry questions, this does not mean that questions located in the other parts of the Question Quadrant have no place in classroom inquiry. Engaging in inquiry places us firmly in the inquiry sector. We are working from there. Even so, we may need to reach out and ask other kinds of questions to assist with our inquiries. These include questions that may be answered in the set material and ones the answers to which can be looked up elsewhere. Open questions that allow us to "brainstorm" possible answers can also be fruitful in inquiry by supplying a list of possibilities to sort through.

FACTUAL, EVALUATIVE, AND CONCEPTUAL QUESTIONS

Inquiry questions can be divided into three basic categories, depending on whether they are factual, evaluative, or conceptual. To put the matter simply, we can say that a factual question is answered by discovering the relevant facts, whereas an evaluative one calls for the justified application of standards or values, and a conceptual question requires an exploration of the meaning or use of key terms.

Each kind of question demands a different kind of response. Students therefore need to be able to distinguish these kinds of questions from one another in order to approach them in the right kind of way. You can assist them to do so by constructing an exercise or two that includes relevant examples of all three kinds of questions in no particular order and asking them to sort them out. The following are exercises of that kind, the first for students in the last years of elementary school and the second for secondary students in history.

Exercise: Facts, Values, and Meanings

Questions to which we don't know the answer are not all the same. Some questions require us to find out the facts. Other questions can only be answered by thinking about our values. Questions can also be asked about the meaning of a word or idea. Sort the following questions into those that are about facts, those that are about values, and those that ask about meanings, by placing the letter *F* for factual, *V* for values, or *M* for meaning, alongside the question.

1. What does it mean to say that North America is a continent?
2. Is North America a larger continent than South America?
3. Would you prefer to live in North America or on some other continent?
4. What is the longest mountain range in North America?
5. What would be the good and the bad things about living in the Rocky Mountains?
6. The Rocky Mountains are said to be a "continental divide." What is that?

Exercise: Sorting Out Inquiry Questions

Identify each of the following questions as primarily factual (*F*), evaluative (*E*), or conceptual (*C*) by placing the appropriate letter alongside each sentence. Be prepared to justify your answer if called upon to do so.

1. What were the main causes of the War of Independence?
2. Were the colonists right to fight for their independence?

3. Should we judge people of earlier times by the standards of today?
4. What are we to understand by the claim that America achieved independence?
5. How many colonies originally formed the United States?
6. Who was Paul Revere?
7. Is Longfellow's poem about Paul Revere's ride partly fictitious?
8. What could it mean to say that history is fiction?

SETTING AN AGENDA

The main purpose of the foregoing is to develop the ability of students to construct their own inquiry questions. In most classroom settings, it is generally better to have students construct questions in small groups, so that they can work on them together, rather than have individuals raise questions. In whatever way you do it, when it comes to bringing these questions together to form an agenda for inquiry, it is a good idea to transfer them directly to the board, so that you can work on them with the class.

Working with students' questions on the board enables you to engage them in sundry tasks, such as elaboration, clarification, spelling, and grammar. More deeply, however, it allows the class to identify the general issues or problems that lie behind their questions and thereby to organize them into a number of potential agendas for discussion. Here is a collection of questions asked by a novice class of students in the first year of secondary school. They were responses to the well-known Heinz dilemma devised by Lawrence Kohlberg.[2]

1. Is stealing OK if no one finds out?
2. Is it ever alright to steal?
3. Is it right to steal from people?
4. Is it OK to break the rules for someone you love?
5. Is it alright to do what's wrong in order to save someone else's life?
6. If you are desperate is it OK to steal?
7. How much is a human life worth?
8. Is it right to do what is wrong when it's right?
9. Is the law always the right thing to follow?

It is easy to see that things like clarifications are required. Are questions 2 and 3 really the same question, for instance, or is 3 more restricted than 2? The play on "right" and "wrong" in question 8 needs to be explored and so on. There are also a number of themes to bring out: the conditions, if any, under which it may be acceptable to steal; following the law and breaking the rules; the value of human life; and the core concepts of *right* and *wrong*. Having got the questions up, the teacher of this class needs to use procedural questioning to help students sort all that out.

Let's look at some thematized questions, again from a class of novices of the same age range. The themes that the class has identified include *Change (C)*, *Growing up (G)*, and *Age and Respect (A&R)*. The questions were asked by individual students and their names were attached for acknowledgment and reference in the lesson. Some of these questions are basically factual and would require engagement in extended research, while others are moral or conceptual questions more suitable for immediate discussion. Which questions go forward also depends on factors such as the curriculum context, student interest, and the time available.

1. How does change occur? (Angela) *C*
2. Do you suddenly grow up or does it happen in stages? (Annie-Kate) *C, G*
3. Why do adults think that what the children have to say isn't important? (Tim) *A&R*
4. What is change? (Serena) *C*
5. How can you change in such a short period of time? (Kris) *C, G*
6. Is anyone superior to anyone else? (Tom) *A&R*
7. Does the way you see things now change when you grow up? (Carlos) *C, G*
8. Why do adults respect other adults more than they do children? (Aaron) *A&R*
9. Why do children have to respect their elders if the adults aren't known to respect the younger ones? (Sharon) *A&R*

UNPACKING PROBLEMS AND QUESTIONS

When we group students' questions to set agendas, they usually revolve around a problem or issue to which the class has responded. When problems or issues need to be explored, we should ask students to first identify them and then pepper them with questions. The word "problem" derives from an ancient Greek word that has the sense of something being thrown before you, and it is worth noting that in Aristotle a problem is seen as throwing a question before you as to the truth or otherwise of a given statement. This has a parallel in talking about things as being problematic in the sense of being questionable.

Let us take a simple scenario that could be used to raise issues as an example. It is the kind of thing that would be suitable for students in their final years of elementary school.

Cindy lives in Los Angeles. Throughout her childhood, Cindy's mother promised to take her to Disneyland, but she never did. So, Cindy decided to save up her pocket money and go to Disneyland anyway. One day, when she was twelve, she told her mother that she was going to spend the day at her friend's house and instead went to Disneyland on her own.

Rather than have students immediately raise questions, we can ask them what issues or problems the passage raises. Obvious candidates include not keeping your promises, lying, and safety. Once students have identified these things, we can go on to have them raise questions for discussion under these headings.

The process of identifying problems and unpacking them through questions leads to work on the questions themselves, whether clarifying and refining them, or attending to aspects of a problem or issue that we initially overlooked. One of the most important moves in working on questions is to raise subsidiary questions. For example, we cannot properly address the question "Can computers think?" without answering the question "What is meant by 'think'?" Unless we address that subsidiary question, we may have no clear conception of what we are claiming computers can or cannot do.

In order to cultivate this practice, it is a good idea to give students an exercise or two in spotting subsidiary questions that relate to questions they raise or that you devise. Here is a simple example: What further questions would need to be addressed in order to properly answer the question of why Pluto is not a planet? Here we would expect students to raise at least the following two questions: What is a planet? What features does Pluto lack that a planet should have? Notice, by the way, that the first question is conceptual while the second is factual. We covered this in the section on Factual, Evaluative, and Conceptual Questions.

THE TEACHER AS PROCEDURAL QUESTIONER

Teachers need to become good at questioning in order to teach students to inquire. Unlike in many other forms of teaching, they do not spend most of their time laying out their subject matter. They devote a good deal of time to questioning students and assisting them to explore relevant problems, issues, and concepts. In doing so, they are not just assisting students to inquire into the matter at hand, but teaching them how to inquire more generally. It is therefore essential that teachers do a good job of questioning.

So far, we have focused on the kinds of questions that form the agenda of an inquiry. Such questions identify problems or issues that arise out of the subject matter being studied. These questions need to be distinguished from those that have to do with the procedures of inquiry. We may label the first kind of questions "substantive" ones. The latter are "procedural." They are the mainstay of teacher interventions in classroom inquiry.

Let's take a simple illustration of the difference between a substantive question and a procedural one.

Teacher: Is fairness a matter of everyone being treated in exactly the same way?
Student: I don't think so—at least, not always.
Teacher: Can you give an example of when it's not fair?

First the teacher asks a question about the nature of fairness. The question specifies the matter for discussion and is therefore substantive. Then a student expresses doubt about whether fairness always demands equal treatment, and the teacher follows up with a question to see whether the student can support that doubt with an example. Here the teacher invites the student to make a particular move—giving an example—to flesh out their initial response. The teacher's question is procedural.

Such questions request students to make particular moves in their thinking as the inquiry proceeds. The basic requirements for the use of procedural questioning in discussion are to listen very carefully to what students are saying and to keep an eye on their overall progress. Unless you do that, there is obviously no way that you can assist them to make much headway. In more detail, you are listening and looking out for a number of things, the most important of which are the following:

Clarity

Is what has been said clear? If not, you need to ask for clarification. Again, it may be clear to you, but not to everyone. You need to look around. Ask other students whether they have understood, or see whether someone can put what was said into their own words. Vagueness is generally more of a problem than ambiguity, but do look out for the latter. Both provide opportunities for students to try to identify the alternative interpretations of what was said.

Relevance

Does what was said contribute to the discussion? If that is not obvious, you may need to ask how it helps. You can assist in maintaining relevance by asking students to build on previous contributions. This includes asking students who agree with what was said to offer something further in support, as well as calling on students who don't agree to say why not. It extends to things like building on what others have said by offering examples, or bringing it into question by suggesting alternative possibilities.

Inquiry-based discussion should make progress in answering the question or questions being addressed. For a contribution to be relevant, it should contribute to this progress. Watch out for the discussion wandering offtrack, or getting bogged down in needless detail. While you don't want to curb enthusiasm by constantly sidelining such contributions, a well-placed question can often assist the class to go back and pick up the thread. Mapping discussion on the board also helps both you and the class to keep track of progress.

Stance

Where do students stand in regard to propositions they raise? Are they being asserted, suggested, or merely put forward as a possibility? Sometimes students will make this clear by the language they use, but you also need to listen out for such things as inflection and tone of voice. If it is not clear where they stand, you need to ask. By the way, don't forget that, even when a student is definitely asserting something, it still has the status of a suggestion within the discussion unless it gains general assent.

Need for Backup

Students will often make comments, or offer opinions, that need support. You should be constantly mindful of this. Be ready to question students to see whether they can supply the class with appropriate evidence, examples, or other reasons, as the case may be. Don't always accept what a student says in response and then pass on. It is often best to keep fishing. Do other students agree with what was said? Are there other—perhaps *better*—reasons to be had? It is vital that students gain a feeling for depth of examination and don't develop a superficial or scattergun approach to inquiry.

Difference and Disagreement

Inquiry depends upon uncertainty as to the outcome. As it proceeds, different possibilities present themselves for consideration, and differing evaluations of them are likely. Rather than skirting around differing views and disagreement, in inquiry they are grist to the mill. If necessary, use questioning to bring them out into the open and to get dialogue going. Intervene with questions to help the class to resolve differences and disagreements through the give-and-take of reasons wherever possible. That is exactly what the evaluation of alternative possibilities in collaborative inquiry requires.

Unnoticed Possibilities

Apart from keeping on top of what is said, listen out for what is not said. It is all too easy for the class to spend time exploring some possibilities while failing to deal with others. Indeed, the class may have failed to bring up things that the teacher was expecting or hoping they would. While care must be exercised in drawing attention to them, they should not be neglected if they are important. Rather than suggesting a possibility yourself, digging around in the area with questions will often help students unearth it. If all else fails, raise the possibility by asking students what they would say to someone who suggested it.

Core Concepts

Look out for concepts that need to be explored. They will be central to the discussion and frequently embedded in what students are saying. Such concepts are usually both complex and a source of contention. Take the concept of fairness, from before. There is often disagreement as to whether something is fair because the disputants are relying on different criteria, or not giving them the same weight. Home in on the concept by asking questions. A good way forward is to raise a scenario where the application of the concept is contentious and question the class about that case. Look at the section on Complex Concepts in chapter 3 for further details.

Assumptions and Implications

Just about anything that is said will rest on assumptions and have implications. Sometimes, however, it may rest on assumptions that are questionable, or have significant implications. Be on the lookout for them and ready to raise questions. What are we assuming here? What follows from that? While teachers should encourage students to make inferences whenever appropriate, dubious assumptions and significant implications provide golden opportunities to encourage inference-making. We will deal with this in detail throughout chapter 4.

The aim of procedural questioning is not just to have students make a particular move on that occasion, but to develop the habit of making such moves when they are needful in working with one another and ultimately when they are thinking something through on their own. This process is greatly aided if the moves are made highly visible. One way of doing this is for teachers to clearly signal them in the language they use and to have students reciprocate by using words that indicate the moves they are making.

This especially applies to procedural questioning in relation to our toolkit. Looking back to the tools listed in chapter 1, you can see that the teacher might ask students to use any one of those tools as the occasion demands, whether to offer a suggestion, give a reason, supply an example, draw an inference, and so on. Here are some illustrations of the various kinds of procedural questions that teachers should ask:

Asking about Questions

- What precisely is the question?
- Are there any other questions that we need to address?
- Can we simply look up the answer to that question or do we need to work it out for ourselves?

Making Suggestions

- Who has a thought about that?
- Does anyone think they know how we can solve that problem?
- Has anyone got a different suggestion?

Giving and Evaluating Reasons

- Can you say why it is so?
- Are there any other reasons that we need to consider?
- Do the reasons in favor outweigh those against?

Providing Examples and Counterexamples

- Can you support what you said with an example?
- Is that an illustration of the kind of thing that Kim was talking about?
- Can you imagine a case where the rule does not apply?

Operations Involving Classification and Division

- What is it that they all have in common?
- Is there a significant difference between these cases?
- How would you define it?

Seeking and Applying Criteria

- Is there some principle or standard that we should apply here?
- Is that the decisive factor?
- When you say that it "all depends," upon what do you think it depends?

Engaging in Thought Experiments

- Can anyone imagine a situation that would help us to think about the problem?
- Let us suppose that really did happen. What would it show?
- How does that scenario support your point?

Thinking about Inferences and Implications

- What does this statement imply?
- Does that follow from what you said?
- What do you think of that argument?

There are three basic ways in which teachers may make tool use explicit through procedural questions.

(1) As we saw earlier, they can be used to call on students to employ a thinking tool:
 Student: The top of the iceberg you can see out of the water and the bottom of it you can't see. So, it's like the top of the culture is more visible than the bottom you can't see.
 Teacher: And can you give us *examples* of some of the things that might be in the more visible section?
(2) Procedural questions can be used to underline the spontaneous student use of a thinking tool by students who are beginning to appropriate it:
 Sam: People have been saying that you should never tell a lie, but what if . . .
 Teacher: Sam is offering us a *counterexample* to the claim that you should never tell a lie. What do others think of that?
(3) They can be used to convert students' comment to tool use, translating students' untutored remarks into appropriate moves in an inquiry:
 Student: That reminds me of what happened last week to my sister. She was . . . .
 Teacher: Are you saying that what happened to your sister is an *example* of the kind of thing we are talking about?

Assisting students to think things through as thoroughly as they can by questioning them often requires the teacher to go on asking questions in order to scaffold a succession of moves in thinking. In the illustration that follows, the teacher's questions are numbered from 1 to 3, picking up on the three kinds of questions mentioned earlier. The relevant thinking tool is identified in italics.

Teacher: What is the *distinction* between a lake and an ocean? Who has a *suggestion*? (1)
Jason: Lakes have fresh water, but oceans are salty.

Teacher: Thank you, Jason. Jason *suggests* that we can distinguish lakes from oceans in terms of fresh water versus salt water. What do the rest of you think of that?
Cindy: You can have a lake with salty water.
Teacher: Can you give us an *example*? (1)
Cindy: The Great Salt Lake in Utah.
Teacher: Thank you, Cindy. We looked at that in our project last term, didn't we? Come to think of it, that's a *counterexample* to the claim that all lakes have fresh water. Do you remember *counterexamples* from last week? Yes? It's back to you Jason. (2)
Jason: OK, but most lakes have fresh water while oceans are always salty.
Teacher: Yes, Amanda?
Amanda: Earlier Jason said that the difference between a lake and an ocean is that one has fresh water and the other has salt water. Now he's saying that lakes don't have to have fresh water in them. That doesn't really work.
Teacher: Are you saying that fresh water *vs* salt water isn't a good basis for the *distinction* between a lake and an ocean? (3)
Amanda: Yes.
Teacher: Jason seems to agree. Are there any other *suggestions*? (1)
Ethan: I was thinking that lakes are surrounded by land, but not oceans.
Teacher: So, lakes have a defining feature that oceans lack. Is that what you're *implying*? (3)
Ethan: Yes, maybe.
Teacher: Hmm, maybe! Yes, Mason?
Mason: I can add to what Ethan said. Lakes are surrounded by land, whereas oceans surround land.
Teacher: Thank you, Mason. That's a nice way of framing a *distinction*. (3)

You can extend your use of procedural questioning to reveal underlying questions and issues through what is known as the Regress of Reasons. The following two snippets of conversation illustrate how the Regress of Reasons works. In them, Thomas keeps asking why he should agree to something.

1.
Mary: You have to go to Julian's party.
Thomas: Why?
Mary: Because you promised him that you would.
Thomas: So?
Mary: You should always keep your promises.
Thomas: Do we *always* have to keep our promises?
2.
Mary: He deserves to be punished for that.
Thomas: Why?
Mary: Because he did something bad, that's why.

Thomas: Do we really have to punish people whenever they do something bad?
Mary: Don't be a pain, Thomas. Both you and I know perfectly well that's right.
Thomas: Do we?

These snippets of dialogue show how quickly a gadfly like Thomas can bring underlying assumptions into question. This is not to say that Mary's assumptions are dubious. Rather, it is to see what is at stake in Mary's claims and to bring these matters forward for consideration by raising questions. Should we always keep our promises? Is it always right to punish bad behavior? These are the kinds of fundamental questions that can readily be unearthed by engaging in the Regress of Reasons.

As indicated in the second of these conversations, it can also be very irritating when you are repeatedly asked to justify what you say. No more so than when questioned about things that you take for granted or are unsure of how to justify. So, when you challenge students by using the Regress of Reasons, it is important for them to know why you're doing it. Tell them that when you repeatedly ask them to justify what they say it is because you want them to dig deeper into the matter and not necessarily to be satisfied with their initial responses.

Yet another technique is to frame questions in terms of one or other of the core areas of philosophy, so as to direct discussion to the metaphysical, epistemological, ethical, conceptual, and logical aspects of the matter in question. When the existence or nature of something needs to be thought about, ask a pertinent metaphysical question. When there is an issue about what is needed by way of evidence, adopt an epistemological posture. When the evaluation of character or conduct is called for, raise ethical questions. The same goes when there is a need for conceptual scrutiny or attention to reasoning.

Obviously, this procedure requires that you have some acquaintance with the kinds of concerns that characterize these areas of philosophy. We will look a little more closely at this matter in a moment to get you started. If you take the trouble to follow it up by further reading or study, you will quickly become alert to the philosophical implications of students' remarks and be prepared to ask corresponding questions.

Let me end these comments with the reminder that collaborative inquiry aims to teach students to think for themselves and that, in this process, the teacher's use of procedural questions is only the first step. While the teacher's procedural questioning assists students to make appropriate moves in their thinking, in order to think for themselves, they need to be able to do so once that scaffolding is removed. Therefore, they should gradually be encouraged to ask procedural questions of one another as well as of themselves.

Observed more closely, the internalization of procedural questioning progresses through three stages in collaborative inquiry:

- First, the teacher uses procedural questions to prompt students to make appropriate moves in their thinking.
- Next, the teacher encourages students to ask such questions of one another. This may be done through targeted activities or exercises as well as in class discussion.
- In the third stage, the social practice of peer questioning is transformed into a self-directed mental habit, as students think about things for themselves.[3] This can be supported by having students engage in self-directed questioning in journal entries and formal written work. It can begin, however, in the early years with a simple activity.

Activity: I Have a Question

Provide each student with a large question mark card which they can hold up during discussion if they want to ask the speaker a question about what they have said. While this can slow down discussion, careful use of the device will help to increase thoughtful interaction between students and avoid the teacher-student-teacher-student pattern in which the discussion is constantly directed through you.

THE CHARACTERISTICS OF PHILOSOPHICAL QUESTIONS

Inquiry in any discipline addresses the kinds of questions that belong in the inquiry question quarter of the Question Quadrant. Since each discipline has its own ways of working, these questions are answered by various means. Some rely on the systematic gathering and analysis of data, others on carefully controlled experiments, and yet others on mathematical modeling, or conceptual analysis and reasoning. Even so, all areas of investigation use the resources of our toolkit. They may be distinguished from one another by the further tools and procedures they employ, but we should not overlook what they have in common.

Given that the specialized disciplines have inherited this core set of tools from philosophy, it is instructive to look at the kinds of questions that drive philosophical inquiry, where those tools do the bulk of the intellectual work. The fact that the tools of philosophy have been designed for such work means that the questions of philosophy provide a natural home for those who are learning to use them. Discussion of such questions provides students with the opportunity to establish basic proficiency that is useful across the curriculum.

While there is always room for debate about what makes a question philosophical, a number of features generally characterize philosophical questions. Let's look at them.

Wide-ranging

Philosophy deals with general questions concerning what exists, what we can know, what we should value, and how we should live. Such questions underlie all sciences and humanities, as well as political, social, and religious thought and practice. Take, for example, the commonplace philosophical question, "What is a good life?" It is a general question that political, social, and religious thought addresses. Again, consider the question, "What is knowledge and how do we come by it?" That question applies to all of the areas of inquiry.

Substantial

Philosophy deals with intellectually and humanly significant questions that lie at the heart of intellectual and cultural life. Substantial as they are, these matters may be neglected by other disciplines or taken for granted in common understanding or cultural practice but not in philosophy. Consider our examples. What constitutes a good life is a substantial question and we may query whether what many people in our society take to be a good life really is good. Among the claims to knowledge are those of science and religion. How those claims bear on one another is a significant intellectual and social issue.

Likely to Remain Intellectually Open

The questions of philosophy tend to be ones that do not admit of a final answer. This does not imply that one answer is as good as any other. Our responses can be life enhancing, clearheaded, and insightful, but they can also be stultifying, muddled, and obtuse. What constitutes a good life, for instance, is not settled for all time, but must perennially remain answerable to the changing conditions in which people live. Again, what constituted knowledge in a traditional society may bear little relation to what we may take it to be in a society transformed by science and technology.

Not Answerable by Empirical Methods

While many open questions can be addressed through empirical investigation, philosophical questions are not able to be answered in this way. This need not mean that everyday experience and scientific knowledge are irrelevant, of course, but they cannot be relied upon to settle such matters. The question of what makes for a good life, for instance, cannot be answered simply by appeal to facts, if for no other reason than that values are involved. Likewise, it may be instructive to empirically investigate what people claim to base their religious knowledge upon, but the justification of those claims cannot be settled in that way.

Addressed through Reasoning and Analysis

While results obtained by other methods of investigation may inform philosophy, it emphasizes careful reasoning and conceptual exploration. Consequently, philosophy has developed the fields of logic and conceptual analysis, from which many of our general-purpose tools derive. To return to our examples, the question of the good life requires us to explore various conceptions of the good in relation to life and engage in argument about such ends as happiness and human flourishing. It cannot also be properly said what knowledge is without analyzing the concept and presenting arguments as to why it is best to conceive of it one way rather than another.

It can be profitable, as well as engaging, for students to be introduced to philosophical questions in terms of the categories into which they are normally divided in philosophy. Here is a small sample of such questions couched in elementary school terms.

Metaphysical Questions

- Do imaginary friends exist?
- What kind of thing is a number?
- What makes the Frog Prince the same person as the Prince before he was turned into a frog?

Epistemological Questions

- If you can see something clearly in your mind does that mean you know it's true?
- Do we have to be able to prove something before we can claim to know that it's true?

- Justin says he knows it, but you said it's just his opinion. What's the difference?

Ethical Questions

- Why is that the *right* thing to do?
- Is it ever OK to lie?
- Was what Maleficent did *wrong* because of the harm she caused or because of why she did it?

Conceptual Questions

- What exactly does that mean?
- Are they the same kind of thing or should we distinguish between them?
- Can you think of any reason someone might have for saying that it isn't fair?

Logical Questions

- What can we infer from that?
- How did you come to that conclusion?
- What are we assuming here?

It can be intimidating to refer to areas of study called "epistemology," "metaphysics," and "logic"—terms with which teachers, let alone students, are not usually familiar. We can avoid such technical-sounding terms, however, without too much damage. Epistemology has to do with knowledge, metaphysics with questions about the nature of things and their identity, while logic is the study of the principles of reasoning.

Other categories present fewer problems. Ethics is the study of morality. Aesthetics deals with questions about beauty and matters of taste. Then there are the philosophies of various fields, such as the philosophy of science, the philosophy of mathematics, the philosophy of language, the philosophy of history, and the philosophy of mind, which are more or less self-explanatory.

The following activity uses headings that should be fine for middle school students. It asks them to divide a group of questions on that basis. One way of running the activity is to distribute a copy of it to students in pairs and, once they have completed the task, to work through the responses with the class, discussing disagreements and uncertainties as you go. With a smaller group of students, you can turn the worksheet into a floor set, by adjusting the font size and printing each heading and question separately. Then you can scatter the headings or questions on the floor and have the students work together to classify them.

With a small group of good students, you can place the questions on the floor and ask them to divide the questions into groups without providing them with headings. When they have sorted out the questions to the best of their ability, you can get them to characterize each group. With a little bit of extra work, you may be surprised how well it will fit the headings, which you can then supply.

Activity: What Kind of Question Is That?

Philosophy asks questions about all manner of things, which we divide into different areas. Four common areas are listed in what follows. There are questions of an ethical nature, questions about knowledge and how we come by it, questions about the basic nature of reality or existence, and questions about what constitutes good reasoning. Together with a partner, see if you can classify the following questions under those headings.

MORALITY KNOWLEDGE REALITY REASONING

- What makes a conclusion justified?
- Could the universe have come from nothing?
- Should we always try to produce the greatest overall happiness?
- Is there anything that we can know for certain?
- Is there really such a thing as a perfect circle?
- What is it to be virtuous?
- Does all of our knowledge come from our senses?
- Is every statement either true or false?
- Does every event have a cause that makes it happen?
- How can we show that an argument is no good?
- Is the mind separate from the body?
- Do we have a duty to help people in need?
- Do we comprehend things more with our minds than with our senses?
- Is doing what is right the same as being good?
- Can we clearly perceive something in our minds and be mistaken?

This brings us back to the point that there are philosophical questions relating to every field of study and the fact that students can benefit from taking a grab bag of questions like the ones set out earlier and dividing them according to school subject areas. All you need to do is to provide them with an assortment of questions separated from the subject groupings and have them allocate the questions. You could run it as a small group activity, followed up by a brief class discussion of the results. Here are suggestions for some school subjects.

English and Language Arts

- Can you have thoughts without language?
- How do words come to have meaning?
- What makes something a poem?
- In what ways can fiction be true?

Social Studies

- What is it for a society to be free?
- Is it wrong for a society to take a person's life?
- What makes for a just society?
- Is democracy the best form of government?

Science

- What is the difference between discovery and invention?
- Are there things that science could never explain?
- Does science provide us with our best guide to what exists?
- Must every event have a cause that makes it happen?

Mathematics

- Do numbers exist in the same way that people and planets do?
- Is there such a thing as a perfect circle, given that no physical thing is perfectly circular?
- How do we know that $5+7=12$?
- Why is mathematics so successful in science?

History

- Can we really know what happened in the past?
- In what ways is history different from science?
- Should we judge people in the past by our own values?
- Is there such a thing as historical progress?

Art

- What makes something a work of art?
- What is the difference between art and craft?
- Is beauty merely in the eye of the beholder?
- Is there a relationship between truth and beauty?

CONSTRUCTING DISCUSSION PLANS

Conducting discussion on the run presents a challenging prospect for many teachers. Nor is it generally desirable. So far as possible, it should be planned beforehand. This is clearly the case when specific aspects of the subject matter need to be covered, or when the topic requires an orderly discussion of a number of key questions. Even a discussion designed around students' questions can be prepared in advance if the questions are raised in one lesson and addressed in the next, allowing the teacher to incorporate them into a Discussion Plan in the meantime.

Discussion Plans are sets of questions that assist teachers and students to examine a topic, issue or problem, in a systematic way. Plans may be sequential, aiming to facilitate a step-by-step exploration of the subject matter by addressing questions about it in a given order. They can also be nonsequential, posing questions in no particular order, while still providing an orderly basis for discussion. They may do so by raising various aspects of an issue, a number of related concerns, alternative possible solutions to a particular problem, or helping to uncover a range of criteria that govern the application of a concept.

Sequential plans often proceed from the textual or concrete to the general or abstract. They may begin with questions that are directly related to a text or other stimulus that provides the raw material out of which problems or issues emerge. Questions that deal with concrete cases or call upon personal experience are often a good starting point. From there the questions can gradually make their way to those that explore a larger context, matters of more general import, or questions that help to bring the cumulative results of the discussion to a resolution or conclusion.

Here are a couple of examples of a sequential Discussion Plan. The first is an elementary school example based on a children's picture book in which a farmer's wife punishes a cat for all the naughty things it did. The second is a junior secondary example based on a photograph of a landless farming family in South Africa living in abject poverty.

Discussion Plan: Dealing with Bad Behavior

1. Did the cat deserve to be punished for what it did in the house?
2. If you had a brother or sister who kept on doing naughty things in your house, what do you think should happen?
3. Does punishing someone for what they did make things right?
4. Is making things right the same as making them better?
5. Could punishments make things worse?
6. In general, how do you think we should deal with bad behavior?

Discussion Plan: Poverty

1. What do you think the life of the people in the photograph would be like?
2. Is it acceptable for people like them to be so very poor, while others in their society are rich?
3. Is it acceptable for some countries to be very poor, while others are rich?
4. Is extreme poverty in a country something that the country should be responsible for dealing with itself, or should the rest of the world help?
5. Do we have a greater obligation to deal with poverty in our own communities than in other parts of the world?
6. What could we do to help reduce poverty in the world?

Let us look at a couple of examples of a nonsequential Discussion Plan. The first one relates to the picture book mentioned earlier. While it draws on incidents in the story, the questions are designed to draw attention to different criteria for fairness and need not follow the plotline. The other is a secondary school example that asks a range of questions about existence in no particular order.

Discussion Plan: Fairness

1. Was it fair for the farmer's wife to put the cat out of the house?
2. Was it fair that the cat was allowed to be in the house when the other animals weren't?
3. Was it fair of the farmer to send the cat out for what it did to his chair when he had let it back in after all the other naughty things it did?
4. Were the other animals fair to the farmer?

Discussion Plan: Existence

1. Does your image in a mirror exist or is it an illusion?
2. Does the past exist?
3. Do numbers exist in the way that physical objects do?
4. In what ways can characters in fiction be said to exist?
5. Does beauty exist in beautiful things or is it just the way we look at them?

EXERCISES AND ACTIVITIES

Question Starters

Activity: Starting Questions with "Should"

The word "should" can be used to raise questions of moral obligation and appropriate or desirable conduct. You can use it as a question starter to assist students to formulate such questions for discussion.

1. Choose a picture book where the conduct of one or more of its characters is clearly questionable.
2. Introduce the word *should* and explain its use in regard to conduct with an example of the following kind: This is how someone behaved. *Should* they have behaved that way?
3. Tell the students that you are going to read them the story and that you want them to be thinking about how the characters in the story behave, so that afterward they will be ready to ask questions about that behavior starting with the word *should*.
4. Read the story and then gather the questions. If need be, work with the class on their proper formulation.
5. Select the best question or questions and hold a brief discussion.

Activity: Raising Questions about Possibilities

The words "can," "could," "may," and "might" can be used to raise questions about possibilities, as in scouting out things that *might* have been responsible, *may* bring something about, *could* explain it, or *can* have that result. You can use these words as question starters to help students raise questions about possibilities for the purposes of elementary inquiry.

1. Select a picture book where something has happened, or happens early in the story, that calls for explanation. It may be something that is later explained, but it could also be something left unexplained in the end.
2. Introduce the words "can," "could," "may," and "might" (or just one or two of them) showing by example how they can be used to raise questions about possibilities.
3. Read the story to the point where something requires explanation. If it is a story where something is ultimately left unexplained, then read it to the end.
4. Have students formulate questions using the words you have introduced for question starters.
5. Conduct a brief discussion to examine the possibilities presented.
6. Where you have left off the story, read it to the end so that the students find out the explanation on offer.

Thinking about Response Demands

Activity: Three Kinds of "Why"

Students need to be able to distinguish between three kinds of Why-questions: questions to which the answers are given, those that they might be able to answer by working on them, and those that they have no prospect of answering satisfactorily.

1. Choose a picture book that will give students plenty of opportunity to ask Why-questions.
2. Explain that after you have read the book, they will have the opportunity to ask a question beginning with "why."
3. Read the story and then record the students' questions. Keep searching around for questions until you have at least one question of each kind.
4. Go through the questions with the class, asking them to decide which of the questions can be answered by going back to the book, which they might be able to answer by working on it, and which ones they are unlikely to be able to settle no matter how hard they try.
5. Test out the categorization of some of their questions by trying to answer them.

Exercise: When Do You Need to Give a Reason?

This exercise can be used as a warm-up for the activity that follows. Start with a sense of collaboration by asking students to complete the exercise in pairs.

Do you need to give a reason for your answers to these questions? Put a tick alongside the question for "Yes" and a cross for "No."

1. Could you be friends with a frog?
2. What is a triangle?
3. Would it be a good idea to spend less time at school?
4. What is your teacher's name?
5. Do you have a sister?
6. Is a dog the best kind of pet?

Activity: When Do You Need to Give a Reason?

1. Work through the students' responses to the previous questions, asking them why they responded as they did when that is appropriate. Use the occasion to encourage students to use the word "because."
2. Engage the class in a brief discussion of the difference between questions where it is appropriate to be called upon to give a reason for your answer and where it is not.
3. Help them to see that some answers require justification because it is open to someone to argue for a different response.
4. Take the question that provoked the liveliest expression of different opinions and discuss it further, stressing reason-giving using "because."

The Question Quadrant

Here are a couple of question sets that can be used with the version of the Question Quadrant designed for the elementary school earlier in the chapter. Simply follow the procedure set out there.

Activity: Questions about Words

1. What is the last word on this sheet?
2. What are some words that express happiness?
3. In what ways does the author of your favorite story use words to make it so good?
4. What changes in spelling did Noah Webster introduce into his American Dictionary?
5. What words can you see on the board?
6. What words can you think of that begin with the letter *W* followed by *h*?
7. Take a line of some poem that you like. How does the poet make it work?
8. The word "music" has its origins right back in ancient Greece. What is the story of that word?

Activity: Questions about Sport

1. Who was Babe Ruth?
2. How important is playing sport for physical fitness?
3. How many different ball games can you think of?
4. What are the rules of football?
5. How many players are there in a baseball team?
6. Are some sports more suitable for boys than for girls, or not?
7. What words might you use to describe an athlete?
8. What were the ancient origins of the Olympic Games?

Let us look at another version of the Question Quadrant. It divides quick-answer and research questions into those that ask students to demonstrate or extend their subject knowledge from questions that require them to apply that knowledge. This results in four kinds of questions: those that can be answered simply by reciting an item of knowledge, those that require students to extend their knowledge by looking up information, those that can be answered by applying their knowledge without much deliberation, and those that require more extended application to work things out. By way of illustration, exercises are provided for geometry and art.

Activity: The Question Quadrant

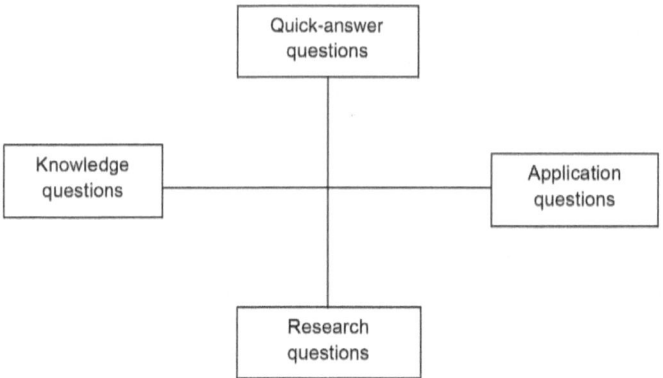

After you have explained this version of the Question Quadrant, hand out a sheet of the questions to students in pairs or threes. Give the students a few minutes to decide where the various questions should go. Then work your way around the Question Quadrant, asking for suggestions about question placement. If there is disagreement or uncertainty, open the matter up for discussion. If time permits, you might like to end by seeing whether your students can suggest additional questions of each kind.

Activity: Question Quadrant (Geometry)

1. What is a rectangle?
2. To what geometrical uses might you put a compass apart from drawing circles?
3. For what advances in geometry is the French philosopher Descartes known?
4. What are the geometrical elements of a geodesic dome?
5. How would you go about drawing up the design for a geodesic dome?
6. How many degrees are there in the internal angles of a triangle?
7. What are some geometrical shapes that you could build out of equilateral triangles?
8. What would the new geometry be like if plane geometry were transferred to the surface of a sphere? (Start by looking at what happens to a straight line as the shortest distance between two points on that surface.)

Activity: Question Quadrant (Art)

1. What are the primary colors?
2. What feelings might you use primary colors to express?
3. Should art have a social purpose?

4. Who painted the *Mona Lisa*?
5. What did Edward Hopper say about how he came to create his painting *Nighthawks*?
6. How were ancient Greek bronze sculptures made?
7. What kinds of elements could you put in a painting to express a sense of calm?
8. How significant was the New York School in the history of twentieth-century art?

Factual, Evaluative, and Conceptual Questions

Students need to be mindful of these different kinds of questions and to develop skill in asking them. We can assist by giving them practice in formulating questions of each kind. Exercises like the following can be done as a whole class, with students making various suggestions about what questions need to be asked and thinking about what makes some suggestions better than others. The first is for elementary school students, while the other two are pitched in turn at the middle and the senior secondary level.

Exercise: Facts and Values

The people below present us with what they take to be the facts, but what they say also raises questions about values. In each case, what do you think is the most important question about values?

Lucas: I can't help it if grandma is upset. All I did was tell her the truth about the jeans she bought me. No one my age wears jeans like that.
Harper: I know that Amy invited me to her birthday party and I didn't invite her to mine. So what?
Oliver: Sure, I punched Jacob. He punched me first.
Amelia: I allowed Cloe to copy my homework only because she is my friend and would have been in trouble for having forgotten to do it.

Exercise: Questions about the Facts

In the cases that follow, we need to know certain facts in order to sort the matter out. In each case, formulate what you take to be the most important question to be asked about the missing facts.

1. After the shooting at the Docklands Gym, police found a revolver in Crusher Morgan's locker.

2. A hitherto unknown painting thought to be by the famous French painter Paul Cezanne has been sent to a laboratory for analysis by art experts.
3. A second will and testament has been produced in the battle for the estate of the late media mogul, Morty Mortlake, further setting family members against one another.
4. Could Anna Anderson of Charlottesville, Virginia, be descended from the Romanov Russian royal family, as she claims?

Exercise: Conceptual Questions

A conceptual question is a question about the meaning or use of words or ideas. What conceptual questions need to be addressed in evaluating the following statements?

1. "Beauty is truth, truth beauty,—that is all/Ye know on earth, and all ye need to know." *John Keats*
2. "You never really understand a person . . . until you climb inside his skin and walk around in it." *Harper Lee*
3. "Deep in the human consciousness is a pervasive need for a logical universe . . . but the real universe is always one step beyond logic." *Frank Herbert*
4. "The world breaks everyone, and afterward, many are strong at the broken places." *Ernest Hemingway*
5. "Do not go gentle into that good night. Rage, rage against the dying of the light." *Dylan Thomas*

Unpacking Problems and Questions

News items provide an abundant source of passages that can be used to give students practice in identifying and articulating problems and learning to ask appropriate questions in order to address them. Here are some examples rewritten from such sources.

Exercise: What's the Problem?

State the nature of the problem raised in the following passage and then ask the basic questions that need to be addressed in order to deal with it.

A recent study has estimated that a vast floating mass of plastic between California and Hawaii has grown to three times the area of France. Dubbed "The Great Pacific Garbage Patch," it contains at least 79,000 tons of discarded plastic, covering an area of about 617,800 square miles. See Scientific Reports, March 2018.

Exercise: What's the Problem?

State the nature of the problem raised in the following passage and then ask the basic questions that need to be addressed in order to deal with it.

New York City authorities have commissioned a monument devoted to the women's rights movement, which is to be installed in Central Park. It depicts two white women, Elizabeth Stanton and Susan Anthony, who played an important part in the struggle to give women the vote back in the nineteenth century. Stanton and Anthony were known, however, to not extend this to African-Americans women. See *The New York Times*, May 14, 2019

Exercise: What's the Problem?

State the nature of the problem raised in the following passage and then ask the basic questions that need to be addressed in order to deal with it.

By the year 2035, according to a recent Census Bureau report, the population of the United States will have "78.0 million people 65 years and older compared to 76.4 million under the age of 18." Never before has the country had more elderly people than minors. See *USC News*, June 21, 2018

Many questions raise other questions. Often these subsidiary questions need to be addressed before we can properly tackle the question with which we began. Giving students practice in teasing out subsidiary questions is a good way of developing the habit of doing so. Here are four examples. The first two are for middle elementary years, while the other two are for language studies and science in the junior secondary years.

Exercise: Questions That Raise Questions

Elijah and Rachael decided to set up a toffee apple stand. Elijah brought along 5 toffee apples and Rachael brought 10 toffee apples, which they put together on a tray. At the end of the afternoon, they had sold all the toffee apples and made $30.

What would be a fair way to divide up the money that Elijah and Rachael made? In order to answer this question, join with a partner and begin by addressing any other questions that you need to think about in order to answer it. Then work out your answer to the original question together with your partner. Be ready to explain how you arrived at your decision and to show your mathematical workings to the class.

Exercise: Questions That Raise Questions

What further questions do you need to consider when attempting to answer the following questions?

1. What is the difference between being just a friend and being a best friend?
2. Can you be best friends with someone for only as long as a mayfly lives?
3. Are the best friendships the ones that last forever?

Exercise: Subsidiary Questions

Read Robert Frost's poem *Mending Wall*. Having regard to the poem, work out what questions need to be addressed in order to properly answer the following question: Do good fences make good neighbors?

Exercise: Subsidiary Questions

What further questions need to be addressed in order to properly answer the following questions?

1. Is a mold a kind of plant?
2. How detrimental are the hazards of molds to human well-being?
3. How important are the benefits we derive from molds for human well-being?
4. What would you say is the most important benefit that we have derived from molds?

Procedural Questioning

Here are some additional activities that you can use to encourage students to engage in procedural questioning.

Activity: Question Cards

Before starting discussion, hand out a number of procedural question cards to reliable students. The writing on the cards should be large enough to be clearly visible across the room. Cardholders are to hold up their card whenever they think the question on it needs to be asked. If they fail to do so when it is needed, subtly signal to them if possible, rather than jumping in yourself. Question cards help the class to take more responsibility for the conduct of their inquiries and help them to internalize the thinking moves that it entails. Here are some generally useful question cards:

- Could you clarify that?
- Does anyone want to ask about that?
- Does anyone have a different suggestion?

- Does anyone disagree with that?
- Who are you responding to?
- Why is that so?
- Can you give an example?
- Does anyone have a counterexample?
- What does that show?
- What are you implying?
- How does that follow?
- What exactly is your argument?

Activity: Q&A

1. Divide the class into pairs, with one person as the questioner while the other is the answerer.
2. Take a discussable topic about which students are likely to hold various opinions.
3. Have the answerers start discussion by expressing their opinion and for questioners to respond with an appropriate question.
4. Give the students a couple of minutes to continue in this way, with the questioner asking further questions to which the answerer responds.
5. Stop the discussion and have the students exchange roles.

Exercise: Do I Do That?

As a reflection on their individual performance, you can have students ask themselves whether they contributed in various ways during class discussion or other collaborative inquiry activities. Having students ask these questions of themselves helps to focus their attention on the various moves in thinking that you are teaching them to make. You can also turn this into a more elaborate response sheet or journal entry by having students identify their strengths and weaknesses and selecting one or two things that they intend to work on in coming lessons. Here is a simple reflection of this kind for younger students.

Did I . . .	YES	NO
point out a problem?		
ask a question?		
make a suggestion?		
offer a reason?		
build on someone's idea?		

NOTES

1. Eric Carle, *The Very Hungry Caterpillar* (New York: World Publishing Company, 1969).
2. See https://en.wikipedia.org/wiki/Heinz_dilemma.
3. The idea that thinking is inner dialogue through questioning is at least as old as Plato: "The soul . . . when it thinks, is merely conversing with itself, asking itself questions and answering them." (*Theaetetus* 189e) It is to Vygotsky, however, that we owe the conception of all the higher psychological functions as internalizations of social practice. See L.S. Vygotsky, *Mind in Society: The Development of Higher Psychological Processes* (Cambridge, MA: Harvard University Press, 1978), 52–57.

Chapter 3

Conceptual Exploration

> We can never achieve command over our thoughts unless we learn how to achieve command over our concepts or ideas.
>
> Richard Paul

When children wonder whether rats are just big mice, or are surprised to be told that whales are not fish, they may feel puzzled or confused. Like them, we are all conceptually uncertain or challenged in this way on occasion, as when we have difficulty categorizing things, making a distinction, or defining our terms. More often, however, most of us pay less attention than we should to the concepts we employ and tend to stumble along conceptually.

The good news is that we can do much to cultivate the conceptual awareness, agility, and expressive powers of our students. As teachers, we can start by developing their proficiency with basic conceptual operations. This chapter will introduce those operations and show how to teach students to use them to do things such as classify, make distinctions, and define terms. We will also see how teachers can help students gain a better understanding of complex concepts by exploring the criteria that govern them. Learning how to do these things will give students a head start in working with ideas.

Let us begin with what is meant by "operations." Piaget used it long ago to refer to actions and mental processes that display a range of characteristics, the most important of which is reversibility.[1] An operation is reversible if it can be carried out in one direction and then again in its reverse. Piagetian operations are, in that sense, binary ones. Simple arithmetic provides obvious examples. Numerical addition has its reverse in numerical subtraction. We can add 3 to 5 to get 8 and then subtract 3 again to return to 5. The same holds for multiplication and division. We can multiply 3 by 5 to get 15 and then we can divide the result by 5 to come back to 3.

While reversibility was emphasized by Piaget, some basic operations come in pairs that are reciprocal rather than reversible. Reciprocal operations deal with relationships that can be read in either direction and are like mirror images of one another. Take "greater than" and "less than," for example. If A is greater than B, then B is less than A. Since their relationship is transitive, the same applies when these relations form a sequence. Thus, if A is greater than B, and B is greater than C, then A is greater than C; and if C is less than B, and B is less than A, then C is less than A.

As mathematical examples illustrate, operations exist within systems. These systems are essential to the acquisition of human knowledge. Indeed, according to Piaget, our knowledge arises out of the assimilation of reality to such systems. Whether or not this is an overly restrictive account of knowledge, there is no denying that organized knowledge of the kind that underpins the school curriculum depends on systems of operations. It is therefore all the more important to attend to them. School education pays a good deal of attention to mathematical operations, of course, but it has tended to neglect conceptual operations in ordinary language.

All conceptual operations involve comparisons. The most elementary comparison involves judging things to be the same or different. Whatever the basis of comparison, if things are regarded as the same in some significant way, then we conceive of them as being in the same category in that respect. If they are judged to be different in that way, we place them in different categories.

Judgments as to whether things are the same or different enter into all *categorical* operations—that is, ones in which we treat things as being of certain kinds or as belonging to classes. They are the basis of classification and division, classical definition, and much distinction-making, all of which involve reversible operations.

Things can also be judged to be to a certain degree similar or different in some respect rather than categorically the same or different. Two people may be tall, but one person *taller* than the other. A team's performance may not be up to scratch and the players need to try *harder*. Adjectives and adverbs such as "taller" and "harder" are said to be *comparative*.[2] Comparative operations, then, are ones involved in comparative judgments. They include comparisons of quantity and degree, ordering things on a scale, and reasoning by analogy. We will come to these operations after we have looked at categorical ones.

CATEGORICAL OPERATIONS

Classification and Division

We can begin to conceptualize something by thinking of it as a thing of some kind. We may think of Little Red Riding Hood as a girl, a grandchild, a character in a fairytale, and so on. In doing so, we assign her to one class or another. That is to say, we *classify* her. Thinking about how she is rescued from the clutches of a villainous wolf by a heroic woodsman, we might become interested in how some fairytale characters are heroes while others are villains. This is to begin to *divide* fairytale characters into groups. The operations of classification and division are the starting point for conceptualization.

In the example above, we began with individual particular things, like Little Red Riding Hood, the wolf, and the woodsman. When we thought about fairytale characters as being of one type or another, however, we were concerned with kinds rather than individuals. As is easy to see, one kind of thing can belong within a larger class of things. Flies are a kind of insect, for instance, just as boots are a kind of footwear. They can also exclude one another, as in things as either organic or inorganic, or either hard or soft. They can also overlap with one another in various ways, as with pranksters and comedians, or festivals and holidays.

Unlike names and expressions that pick out individual particular things, notice that common nouns, like "fly" and "boot," denote kinds of things. Most categorical conceptualization and a good deal of reasoning depend on operations using common nouns to capture relations between various kinds of things. Giving students practice in identifying these relations will help them to prepare for what is to follow. Here is an exercise that paves the way for classification. It is suitable for middle elementary school.

Exercise: Kinds of Kinds, of Kinds, and so on

1. Tell your students that they are going to think about kinds of kinds of things. Give them an example, such as a poodle is a kind of dog and a dog is a kind of animal.
2. Ask them to name some of the varieties of the things on the list, such as lounge chairs, ladybugs, or teaspoons.
3. Ask them to name a more general kind to which each of the things on the list belong, such as beetles being a kind of insect.
   - Boots
   - Apples
   - Planes
   - Chairs

- Beetles
- Spoons
4. If students find the task easy, see if they can take it one step further, as in a poodle is a kind of dog, a dog is a kind of animal, and an animal is a kind of living thing!
5. Now start with very general kinds of things, such as the following:
   - Animals
   - Plants
   - Tools
   - Buildings
   - Games
6. Ask someone to name a kind of thing that falls under the first item on the list. For animals, it might be bears.
7. Now ask for a kind that falls under it—polar bears, let us say, as a kind of bear. Try out different suggestions.
8. Where possible, see whether someone can take it one step further—as in a spade being a kind of gardening tool.

Let us review what has been said about basic categorical operations. A kind of thing generally can be divided into various sub-kinds. This is called "division." For example, we might divide living things into animals and plants. While this results in a simple classification scheme, the operation of classifying is the inverse of dividing. To classify something is to assign it to a class of a more general kind. Thus, we classify animals and plants when we place them under the category of living things.

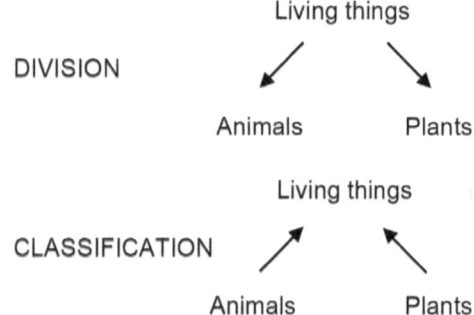

Recalling what was said about basic operations in arithmetic, notice that the relationship between classification and division is analogous to that between addition and subtraction. Grouping things together and separating them comprise a pair of operations in much the same way as adding things on and taking them away. When adding on and taking away are enumerated, we get addition and subtraction. When grouping things together and separating them are conceptualized, we get classification and division.

Being able to employ the elementary operations of classification and division is as basic in learning to think conceptually as is mastering addition and subtraction in learning to think mathematically. Since the ability to think conceptually is no less important than the ability to think mathematically, learning to classify and divide should also be an essential part of children's education. Young children should be expected to achieve proficiency in the elementary operations of conceptualization just as in the elementary operations of arithmetic.

Let us take a couple of elementary school exercises that introduce division. The first involves assigning lists of things to categories. The other involves dividing playthings into groups. The same activities can be carried out by replacing the lists with a variety of other kinds of things with which your students are familiar.

Exercise: Two Kinds of Things

Supply students with the following lists of words and have them work in pairs to divide each list into two groups of things that belong together.

1. knife, breakfast, spoon, lunch, fork, dinner
2. shoe, jeans, boot, shirt, coat, slipper
3. chair, cupboard, drawer, stool, bench, wardrobe

This need not mean having a word for each group. Depending on their age, students might not have a word like "cutlery," for example, but simply talk about "things you eat with." That's fine. Constructing a descriptive phrase to define a category does the same conceptual work. Once they've done this, it may be a good time to introduce a word such as "cutlery." Also, sometimes there is no common name for a category. While "seat" names one group in the third list, for instance, we don't have a word for the other group. Students might talk about "furniture in which to store things" instead.

Exercise: Playthings

playing cards	Barbie doll	toy truck	rocking horse	baseball bat
model train	dart board	fluffy bear	doll house	skateboard
dice	beach ball			

1. Make copies of the set of playthings on cards (adding clipart if you like) so that each group of three or four students can be given a set.
2. Distribute the sets, telling the class that the playthings are to be divided into groups. They can have as many groups as they like, except that one plaything all by itself is not a group. Also say that they will need to be able to name or explain each group.

3. When the task has been completed, ask a couple of groups with different groupings to explain what they have done.
4. Encourage the class to challenge any grouping, or placement of a plaything in a group, if they think there is a problem. Ensure that students give reasons for what they say and, when appropriate, open the matter up for wider discussion.

The previous exercise began with a list of things under the general concept of *playthings* and asked students to divide them into various subcategories. It resulted in an elementary classification scheme for the things on the list. In more complicated schemes, we may begin this way, but then proceed to further divide the kinds that fall under those subcategories and continue on down, as the case demands. Here is a challenging exercise of that kind for junior secondary students. It is about games, but you can use any collection of things that suits your subject matter, such as animal species, landforms, artworks, geometric forms, and so on.

Exercise: Games

Football	Chess	Basketball	Dominoes	Golf
Hockey	Scrabble	Tennis	Soccer	Tenpin Bowls
Table Tennis	Baseball			

1. Divide the class into groups of no more than four and provide them with the list of words under the general category of *games*, together with a large sheet of paper and a marker. They should also have a separate piece of paper in order to try things out before committing themselves to writing up their work on the large sheet.
2. Starting with the word "Games" at the top of their sheet, the group's task is to name the different kinds of games listed, drawing a separate line down from the word "Games" for each kind of game identified.
3. Where appropriate, they should divide the kinds of games already identified into further subcategories, naming those subcategories as they proceed down the page. The result should be an inverted treelike structure, with the words on the list placed at the ends of the branches.
4. Have one or more groups present their classification scheme to the class and engage in discussion of any problems or ways of improving what they did.

Here are things to watch for as you help guide discussion of students' efforts:

- *Are the categories mutually exclusive?* If an item can be listed on more than one branch, then the divisions overlap and students should avoid it. If we had *field games* going down one branch and *ball games* going down another, for

instance, then a game such as football would end up listed under both *ball games* and *field games*. Here we might replace *ball games* with *court games* (like tennis). Then football would fall under *field games*, with no overlap.
- *Are the differences between divisions significant ones?* Fields and courts are not just distinct from one another. The games in question are distinctive in being played on one rather than the other. Nor will they overlap with games played on a board, board games once again being significantly different in this respect.
- *Are the categories in the scheme jointly exhaustive?* A classification scheme should not omit anything of the kind in question. In the exercise from earlier, we are only concerned with the games listed and obviously none of these should be omitted. An exhaustive classification scheme of games, however, would have to cater for those that are not on the list.

Conceptual Opposition

Opposites provide a familiar way in which to conceive of things. They involve differences in kind that are poles apart, as we might say. The following device gets younger students thinking in terms of opposites by building up families of words. It begins with a pair of antonyms and then successively calls for synonyms and antonyms to build up the weight on each side of the dumbbells. It can be applied to all kinds of opposites where students can be expected to have a range of associated vocabulary.

Exercise: Dumbbells

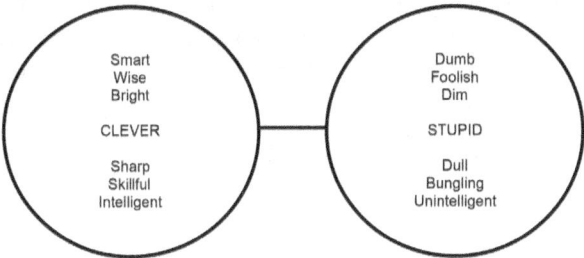

1. Write the words for a pair of opposites in the circles of the dumbbell, as in CLEVER and STUPID in the illustration.
2. Ask your students to think of another word that is similar in meaning to one of the words. When a word is suggested, place it in the appropriate circle and see whether someone can suggest its opposite. Keep going backward and forward until the class runs out of words.

You can also provide students with the vocabulary associated with a selected conceptual opposition and ask them to sort out the words. In the following example, notice that there is a question mark. It means that students are uncertain in which category to place a word. If the task is carried out in pairs or threesomes, it can also mean that individuals think they know in which group the word should go, but they disagree with one another. Make sure to discuss uncertainties and disagreements.

Warm-up Activity: Free

Sort out the words below into those that belong with *Free* and those that go with *Not free*. If you aren't certain about a word, then place it under the question mark.

| Free | ? | Not Free |

constrained   optional   restricted   compulsory   unavoidable
permitted   obligatory   trapped   released   involuntary   forced
liberated

Dichotomous Division

In dichotomous division we separate the things that have a nominated property from everything else in a category. With games, for example, we might divide off board games from all the other games, which are not board games. This division is of the form *X/not-X*.

Such a division is guaranteed to be both mutually exclusive and jointly exhaustive of the category in question—making dichotomous division a way of going about logical division. We may continue to divide the remainder of the category (the *not-X* part) by applying the same operation as many times as necessary. Here is the partly worked out example of games from an earlier exercise set out as a dichotomous division.

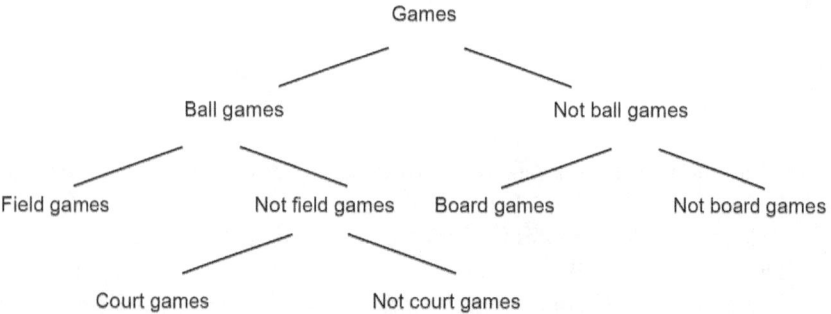

Take care not to confuse dichotomous division with the kind of conceptual opposition marked by antonyms. Dichotomous division divides the whole of a category into two mutually exclusive and jointly exhaustive groups. Antonyms are mutually exclusive, but they are not usually jointly exhaustive. The opposite of "tall" is "short," for instance, and it is possible to not be tall without being short. Problems can arise for the unwary, however, due to the fact that sometimes *X/not-X* represents such oppositions rather than dichotomous division. The following is an exercise designed to alert students to this fact.

Exercise: Can You Pick the Opposites?

Which of the following are opposites? Where they are not opposites, can you say what the opposite would be and provide an example to prove that they are not opposites—as for instance, someone who is not tall without being the opposite of tall?

Tall	Not tall
Correct	Not correct
Young	Not young
Honest	Not honest
Beautiful	Not beautiful
True	Not true

Distinctions

We see the need to make a distinction when things have been regarded as the same, or are in danger of being treated that way, but we want to argue that they are significantly different. In making distinctions we are therefore dealing with sameness and difference, the very things involved in the categorical operations of classification and division. Consequently, it is useful to have students begin by identifying the general kind to which the things to be distinguished belong—the basic move in classification. Encourage them to be as precise as possible, by looking for the most specific general kind that includes both things.

Having identified as precisely as possible the general kind of thing with which they are dealing, students need to work out how to divide the particulars in question from one another. It needs to be stressed that they are not looking for incidental differences, but for the most distinctive or relevant ones. It is important to note that the differences in question can be comparative rather than categorical ones—something that we will attend to later. For now, we will stick with cases where the differences are one of a kind.

The combination of these two operations helps students to relate distinction-making to division and classification. It involves a division between things that belong to a more general kind under which they can be classified. Understanding that distinction-making builds upon what are by now familiar categorical operations will make it easier for students to learn to make distinctions, and as they progress, seeing how to employ those operations in various conceptual tasks will strengthen their overall conceptual capability.

Exercise: Drawing Distinctions

- Slippers and shoes
- Planes and helicopters
- Tunnels and caves
- Prisons and forts
- Hopping and jumping
    1. Begin by explaining what is required by way of a simple example. Suppose, for instance, that in dining we were going to distinguish between table knives and forks. First, we ask: What are they both? It could be said that they are both tableware, or perhaps things you eat with. More exactly, of course, they are *cutlery*. Then we ask: As cutlery, how do knives and forks differ? Again, we might point out all sorts of differences, but one basic difference is that knives are used for cutting food whereas forks used for raising it to the mouth.
    2. Now introduce one of the pairs above and work with the class on making a distinction in two steps, as before, beginning with the question, "What are they both?" before turning to the question, "How do they differ?" (It is best to begin with cases where we have a word for the general kind, as in *footwear* and *aircraft*.) Encourage students to discuss proposals and try to refine them where appropriate.
    3. Select something else from the list and have the class work in pairs to make the distinction, reminding them that they first need to identify what makes the two things the same kind of thing before they look for the difference between them.
    4. Now turn to class discussion. Don't allow the class to move on to a different suggestion until the one under discussion has been carefully considered. This is an opportunity to engage students in critical and creative thinking.
    5. Continue in the same way for the other pairs, as time permits.

You can base a whole lesson on distinction-making, starting with an exercise to focus on the topic to warm-up the class. The following example begins with a warm-up that distinguishes the vocabulary that we may use when we say a person knows something from other words that don't measure up. The Discussion Plan that follows it focuses on the distinction between knowing and believing.

Exercise: Do You Know It or Not?

Which of the words below can be fitted into the blank in the following sentence and which of them don't really do the job?
If you _____ something, then that counts as knowing it to be true.
prove   remember   imagine   discover   see   assume   realize
believe   detect

Discussion Plan: Knowing and Believing

1. If you know something, does that mean you must believe it?
2. If you believe something, does that mean you must know it?
3. Can you believe something for which you lack adequate reasons or evidence?
4. Can you know something for which lack adequate reasons or evidence?
5. Can you believe something even though it isn't true?
6. Can you know something even though it isn't true?

Definition

We now turn to the traditional way of constructing a definition that goes all the way back to the ancient Greek philosopher Aristotle. Following Aristotle's way of doing things, definition involves identifying the general kind to which something belongs and the distinctive feature or features that mark it off from other things of that kind. Thus, dinner knives are pieces of cutlery (general kind) that are used for cutting food (distinctive feature).

This way of constructing definitions utilizes the operations of classifying and dividing that we employed in making distinctions. We classify whatever we are trying to define under the general kind that provides the best fit. Then we identify what is distinctive about it by contrast with other things in that category. This means that, once students have satisfactorily made a distinction, you can ask them to construct a definition in the Aristotelian way. Have them recall the two ingredients and put them together in a sentence. For example, "A cave is a *natural* (distinctive feature) *underground chamber* (general kind)".

Things that can be adequately defined in this way involve what we may call "simple concepts." It is important to note that many concepts cannot be captured by such a straightforward way. They are far more complicated than that. This particularly applies to concepts that are central to our understanding of everyday life, such as our ideas of friendship, fairness, and freedom. Such concepts may be analyzed, but they elude clear-cut definition. We may call them "complex concepts"—something we will come to later in the chapter.

Categorical Comparisons

In the simplest cases, we compare things because they have some property in common. Football and baseball are alike in being field games, for example, and different in that respect from basketball and tennis, which are played on a court. Similarly, 5 and 7 are alike in being odd numbers. They are different in that respect from 6 and 8, which are even. Such comparisons are equivalent to classification.

Students need to see that they are relying on familiar operations in making such comparisons. A simple exercise can be used to make the point.

Exercise: Being Alike

In what way are the following pairs basically alike?

Grandmother/Grandfather
Cup/Mug
Bicycle/Motorbike
Square/Circle
Telescope/Magnifying glass

When we compare things in this way, we pick out a significant common property or properties and ignore the rest. Consider customary similes, such as being as quiet as a mouse or as cute as a button. The things compared need have no significant features in common other than the one in question. Analogies are similar. When it is said that it was as if a man in trouble had walked into quicksand—the more he struggled the deeper he sank—we equate certain features of the two situations and disregard the others.

All forms of analogy share this feature. Consider the classical form of analogy "*A* is to *B* as *C* is to *D*," as in "mother is to daughter as father is to son." The parallel is easy to see. A mother is a parent of her daughter, just as a father is a parent of his son in being same-sex parent-child relations. Once you have introduced students to this form of analogy with an example, you can give them exercises such as the following to complete in pairs or threesomes.

Exercise: Likeness between Pairs

In what way are the following pairs alike?

IN and OUT/UP and DOWN
LEFT HAND and RIGHT HAND/The letters *p* and *q*
LETTER and WORD/WORD and SENTENCE

    Students may find the exercise challenging. Don't forget to remind them that they are working with the classical analogical form "*A* is to *B* as *C* is to *D*". In that form, "IN is to OUT as UP is to DOWN" presents us with opposite directions; "The left hand is to the right hand as *p* is to *q*" presents pairs that are mirror images of one another; and "Letter is to word as word is to sentence" are both part-whole grammatical relations.

These classical analogies cannot always be analyzed in one step. Consider "a pair of crutches is to a walking stick as a pair of glasses is to a monocle." While the pattern of two-to-one is obvious, we need to identify a more general kind to which all these things belong and under which we can distinguish between two sub-kinds that can be divided in a parallel fashion. In this case, they are all aids, one pair for walking and the other for sight, each pair being divided again into a singular and double support.

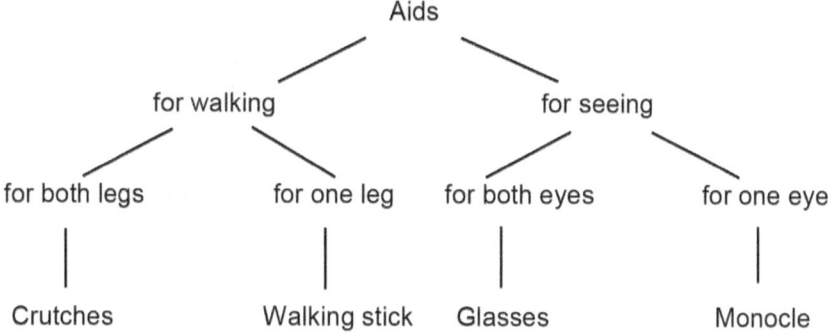

    As you can see, this comparison is nothing more than distinction-making carried out through parallel division. As with simpler analogies, it provides another illustration of how conceptualization employs the same basic operations for many different purposes. Working out the parallel distinctions involved in such analogies can provide a more challenging exercise for students who have mastered the simple ones.

COMPARATIVE OPERATIONS

In coming to comparative operations, we need to remember that, while all conceptual operations involve comparisons, we are using the term "comparative operations" to refer to operations involved in judgments that employ adjectives and adverbs such as "smaller," "better," and "harder" that are said to be *comparative*. To say that gold is harder than lead, for instance, is to make a comparative judgment. Conceptually speaking, it involves comparing gold and lead by ordering them on a scale or gradation of hardness. Comparative operations, then, are ones underpinning comparative judgments.

While we are all familiar with comparative judgments, it is worth making some remarks about them before getting into action. Like their categorical cousins, comparative judgments involve two-way relations. If Mandy is *faster* than Andy, then Andy is *slower* than Mandy. If Mandy arrived *earlier* than Andy, then Andy arrived *later* than Mandy.[3]

The difference, however, is that comparisons of this kind turn on the *relative* likeness of things, or the *comparative* difference between them. They involve what we might call "shades-of-gray" judgments, as when we note a family resemblance, or improvement in a student's work. They operate in different ways from categorical ones, and so we need to be aware of the terms in which we conceive of things and mindful of whether the situation calls for categorical or comparative judgment.

Students are called on to make comparisons throughout the curriculum, from working with comparative language in language arts, to using rankings and bar graphs in science, and working with symbols such as ">" and "<" in math. They are put to work, whether in analyzing poems, recording observations, or solving mathematical problems. Given the widespread reliance on them, we should make an effort to develop students' general understanding of comparative operations.

Introducing Comparative Language

When you start work on comparisons, particularly with elementary school students, be sure that they know how to identify common comparative words by the addition of telltale "er" or "ier" suffixes, as in: "tall/taller," "round/rounder," "fast/faster," "early/earlier," "silly/sillier".

You should also not neglect superlatives, as in "tallest," "roundest," "fastest," "earliest," and "silliest," as they also involve comparisons. The silliest behavior, for instance, is sillier than all the other behavior with which it is compared.

Introductory vocabulary exercises for younger students can be followed up by ones that ask them to distinguish between categorical and comparative statements, as in the following:

Exercise: Making Comparisons

To say that Glenda is tall is simply to state something about Glenda, whereas to say that Glenda is taller than Rachael is to make a comparison. Which of the following people are making comparisons?

Weather Man: Tomorrow will be colder than today.
Student: My desk is tidy.
Child: My grandmother is the oldest member of our family.
Coach: You can run faster than that.
Dog Owner: He is just a puppy.
Teacher: The class needs to be quieter.

Ordinal Comparisons

Just as we can assemble families of words using conceptual opposition, so we can order vocabulary under a concept by making comparisons. Consider the concept of temperature. We can order words that have to do with temperature along an ordinal scale. The easiest way to do this is to draw a line and place "coldest" at one end and "hottest" at the other. The line then represents a bridge between the two—or between whatever opposing superlatives are appropriate for the concept in question. Here is an exercise of that kind.

Exercise: Bridge

Concept: Temperature

1. Place the superlative terms for a concept at the ends of a line and ask the class to name the concept.
2. Position one or two words along the line and then invite students to supply words that fall somewhere along it. Start with your marker at one end and begin moving along the line, asking the student who suggests a word to stop you when you get to where it belongs.

3. Add the word and then repeat the procedure until the class runs out of words.
4. Be sure to discuss any uncertainty or disagreements.

As an alternative procedure, you can lay a cord on the floor and label it as you would on the board. Then hand out a list of words that fall along the line to pairs or small groups of students and have the class try to place their words in order. Here is a set of words for describing the local temperature from the coldest to the hottest: freezing, frosty, cold, cool, mild, warmish, warm, hot, sweltering, and sizzling.

While ordering vocabulary along the line is a comparative operation, it is important to remember that each individual word is categorical when considered by itself, even if the category is ill-defined. It is one thing for the temperature to be warm, for example, and another thing for it to be hot. We also commonly divide ordinal ranges into categories for the purposes of judgment, or make use of numbers to divide a variable into categories Thus, temperatures are said to be below freezing when a thermometer reads below 32° F, for example, and to be above boiling point at plus 212° F.

Comparisons of Quality and Quantity

It is customary to distinguish between comparisons based on quality and quantity. Consider the following comparisons: "All that glitters is not gold," "The Unites States currently produces 230 tonnes of gold a year by comparison with Canada's 176 tonnes." The first warns us about being deceived by appearances that may mask differences in underlying *quality* while the second compares the *quantity* of gold produced by two countries.

The distinction between quantity and quality is fundamental. Scientific comparisons are basically quantitative. Comparisons in the arts are usually qualitative. Correspondingly, some school subjects tend to rely on quantitative comparisons and others on qualitative ones. It is of note, however, that both kinds of comparisons are in everyday use, often in conjunction with one another. When considering a purchase, for example, you might shop around to compare prices, at the same time comparing the quality of the items on offer.

The following is an exercise for more advanced secondary students that asks them to distinguish between these two kinds of comparisons.

Exercise: Comparisons of Quantity and Quality

In each of the following cases, say whether the comparison involved is one of quality or of quantity.

1. A bird in the hand is worth two in the bush.
2. To err is human, to forgive, divine.
3. There are more stars in the heavens than grains of sand on earth.
4. The pen is mightier than the sword.
5. An ounce of prevention is worth a pound of cure.
6. Shall I compare thee to a summer's day?

Examining the Basis of Comparisons

Some kinds of comparisons are more precise than others. In the case of temperature, considered earlier, standardized measuring instruments enable us to use a numerical scale to mark differences numerically and that provides us with a well-defined and objective method of comparing temperatures. Although not all comparisons have that kind of precision, that is no excuse for sloppy thinking and there are things we can do to avoid it.

Suppose someone says that one proposed course of action is far more sensible than another. We might ask them why that is so and consider their reasons. The main thing to look for in whatever justification they offer is the respect, or respects, in which the actions are being compared. That will be the basis upon which their claim stands or falls. It enables us to judge whether the difference between the proposals justifies the claim that was made.

Here is a simple example. Donald suggests that it is far more sensible to put on sunscreen than simply wearing a hat when going to the beach in summer. When asked why that is so, he says that sunscreen protects all areas of the skin to which it is applied, whereas a hat protects only the head. The extent of the skin protected is clearly the basis of Donald's comparison. Being clear about the basis of comparison puts us in a better position to evaluate his claim, which looks to be reasonable in that far more of the skin can be protected by sunscreen than by a hat. It might be even more sensible to wear both sunscreen and a hat, of course.

Here is an exercise that encourages students to uncover the basis of a comparison that is used to make a claim.

Exercise: Reasoning with Comparisons

The following people are making a claim based on a comparison between two things. What is the basis of their comparison and how well does that support their claim?

Cindy: It is better to walk to school than to catch the school bus. That way you get lots of exercise.

Pete: Look at all that ice in Antarctica. There isn't nearly so much ice in the Arctic. It must be much colder in Antarctica than in the Arctic.

Nutritionist: Hamburgers are healthier than donuts. The average hamburger has only half the fat content of a donut.

Grumpy: You can't tell me that those trees are lovelier in fall than in summer. Look at all the leaves I have to rake up every day in the fall.

COMPLEX CONCEPTS

Two and half thousand years ago, Socrates tried to discover features that are common to all things good, or just, brave or beautiful. In other words, he attempted to discover the nature of the general kind to which such things belong. Plato's *Dialogues* show Socrates striving but failing to reach his goal. This may be because there are no common criteria that distinguish all the cases to which such complex concepts are applicable. As the twentieth-century philosopher Ludwig Wittgenstein remarked, the criteria that govern the application of such concepts may vary from one case to another because they are related by nothing more than a family resemblance.

Such concepts have a complicated logical geography. It is not always easy to say whether someone counts as a friend rather than an acquaintance, for instance, or whether an outcome really is just. The same applies to saying that an action was brave rather than foolhardy or that something is beautiful and not just pretty. We may appeal to a number of things in making these judgments and be uncertain how to weigh them in the balance.

This complexity also means that there can be room for disagreement as to what should be said in one case or another. Haley may say that there was nothing wrong with giving her young sister a smaller piece of the birthday cake because she is just little, while her sister complains that it wasn't fair because she was given a smaller piece than everyone else. The girls are appealing to conflicting criteria in order to justify their judgments.

Having students attend to the criteria that govern the application of complex concepts markedly increases their understanding of them and ability to apply them. This is true even of far simpler concepts than the ones above. Someone might attempt to distinguish hopping from jumping, for example, by saying that hopping is done on one foot, whereas jumping is done with both feet. The number of feet involved is their suggested *criterion* to distinguish hopping from jumping. If someone else points out that birds hop on two feet, then they are arguing against using that difference as a general criterion for distinguishing between the two.

Paradigm and Contrary Cases

If students are not already familiar with the notion of a criterion, you can introduce it by drawing attention to its use in distinction-making and definition. Use the opportunity to ground this new term in practices that are already familiar. You can then go on to develop the capacity to identify and explore the criteria that govern more complex concepts through the use of *paradigm* and *contrary* cases.

Paradigm Cases

Let us take a paradigm case of lying, for illustration. Suppose that Jamie snatched Angela's pen from her desk, but when asked about it by the teacher, he said that he didn't do it. This looks to be a clear case of lying. Examination of the case will begin to reveal what is involved in lying. Jamie said that he didn't do something, when he knows that he did. What he says isn't true. That is part of what makes it a lie.

Contrary Cases

These are related cases in which the concept does not apply. As such, they draw attention to significant requirements that fail to be met. Let us go back to Jamie. Saying something that isn't true is not the only thing involved in lying. It is important to note that Jamie *knowingly* said something that isn't true. Suppose that he took Angela's pencil thinking that it was his own. When challenged by the teacher, he says that he didn't take Angela's pencil. Here what Jamie says isn't true—he did take Angela's pencil—but doesn't *know* it. So, he isn't lying.

While the concept of lying isn't very complicated, more is involved than students might have thought. Examining a paradigm case together with one or more contrary cases will help to reveal the criteria that govern it. To extend the illustration, consider the following exercises on stealing and cheating. They begin with a paradigm case, asking students to discuss what it is about the case that makes it clear that the concept applies. Then, they present a couple of contrary cases, where it is more or less clear that the concept does not apply. The contrary cases help to bring out aspects of the concept that may have been missed.

Exercise: Is That Stealing?

In the following cases, did Brendon steal Angela's yoyo? If so, why is it stealing and, if not, why?

1. Brendon took Angela's yoyo and put it in his bag, but then denied it.
2. Brendon put Angela's yoyo in his bag thinking it was his own yoyo.
3. Brendon put Angela's yoyo in his bag because she said he could borrow it.

Exercise: Was He Cheating?

In the following cases, was Roberto cheating? If so, why is that cheating? If not, why?

1. Roberto won the game by sneakily swapping some of his cards with ones on the table.
2. Roberto won because some of his cards got mixed up with those already on the table.
3. Roberto won because he was allowed to swap some of the cards with those already on the table.

Borderline Cases

Unlike paradigm and contrary cases, where a concept clearly applies or does not apply, a borderline case is one in which it is arguable whether or not the concept applies. Borderline cases are therefore likely to provoke conflicting responses and stimulate discussion. If Brendon took Angela's yoyo and put it on his desk, for example, has he stolen it? The case is arguable. If Roberto won the game because he caught a glimpse of the cards that someone else was holding, we might want to know more before we rush to judgment.

Roberto's case helps to bring at an important point. Often students respond to borderline cases by suggesting that it "all depends." This means that they are sensitive to criteria that may apply, but cannot say whether they do so in this case without more detail. Take the opportunity to ask them what they think it depends upon and why it depends on that. This will bring out the criteria that they have in mind.

We have seen that students can begin to discover the criteria that underlie complex concepts by examining a variety of scenarios with which they are familiar. As with many of the judgments that we make in life, some of these cases may be hotly contested. Such conflicting judgments need not be due to self-interest or bias. We do not judge all cases of fairness by the same criteria, for example, and people may apply somewhat different criteria or weigh them differently.

The following activity, which explores the concept of fairness, may be rerun for any complex concept by constructing an appropriate range of scenarios and following the same procedure. Because the matters to which such concepts apply are complex and variable, it is important to bear in mind that the objective is not so much to achieve general agreement about particular cases, as to become clear about the criteria that apply.

Concept Game: Fairness

Here is a set of scenarios:

- Since Jasmine's brother is older than she is, he is allowed to stay up later than her.
- Although Natasha ate more than her share of the birthday cake, there was plenty for everyone.
- Uncle James is fonder of Jackson than of his sister. So, he always gives him a better present at Christmas.
- Since Tim wasn't very good at races, he was allowed to start before everyone else.
- As no one would own up to having made the mess, the whole class was made to clean it up.
- Nick knew who had broken the chair, but wouldn't tell. So, he was the one who got into trouble.

Now proceed as follows:

1. Tell the class that in this activity they will be thinking about fairness. Draw up three columns on the board labeled "FAIR," "NOT FAIR," and "?" leaving a space at the left to list the cases to be discussed (e.g., allowed to stay up later).
2. Explain that the "?" means that we're not sure whether something is fair or aren't generally agreed as to whether or not it's fair. (To say that we aren't agreed implies that, as a group, *we* are not sure, even if some individuals are sure.)
3. Divide the class into small discussion groups, explaining that you will read out a scenario and give them a minute or two to discuss whether what happened was fair. Make it clear that they will need a good reason for whatever they decide. If they cannot agree, they will need to be able to explain the reasons for that.
4. Read out a scenario and then give the groups time to discuss whether what happened was fair, and why or why not.
5. Stop the discussion, read out the scenario again, and call on a group who agreed with one another to say what they think. Record their essential point or points in the appropriate column on the board, trying to capture as succinctly as possible the criterion they rely on to make their judgment.

6. Ask whether others would like to add to what was said or to express disagreement with it. Record the main points on the board.
7. Do the same for the other scenarios.
8. End the activity by having the class help you to underline the key points on the board. If time permits, engage in a round-robin to give students the opportunity to briefly comment on something they discovered about fairness or on anything about it that still puzzles them and needs sorting out.

CLARIFICATION

Clarity has sufficiently close ties to conceptualization to merit some remarks here. Clarification is called for when students fail to adequately express their thoughts because of ambiguity or vagueness. Ambiguity arises when an expression has more than one meaning, leading to different interpretations of what is being said, while vagueness comes from students not making their meaning sufficiently precise. Although vagueness is a far greater problem than ambiguity, it is worth drawing attention to ambiguous expressions, if only to have students exercise their ability to analyze language.

Ambiguity

Consider Groucho Marx's humorous remark: "Time flies like an arrow; fruit flies like a banana." Employing grammatical analysis or alternative unambiguous restatements to disambiguate such a remark can be both instructive and enjoyable. With a little effort, you can construct your own exercises in which students reword ambiguous sentences to make the speaker's meaning clear, as in the following example.

Clarification: Can You Say That Again?

The statements below suggest something that the speaker did not intend. Work with your partner to rewrite the statements so as to make the intention clear, making as few changes as possible.

1. When Mary was over at Jane's house, she gave her cat food.
2. Parents should include their children when baking cookies.
3. Safety experts say that children on school buses should be belted.
4. The cyclist hit the old man with a walking stick.
5. For those who have young children and don't know it, we run an after-school program.

The same can be done with ambiguities that make reasoning go astray. The technical name for this is the Fallacy of Ambiguity. Dealing with it requires students to reword one or more of the premises, so as to capture their meaning in such a way as to make it clear that the conclusion does not follow.

Clarification: That Doesn't Follow!

Something has gone wrong in the following examples of reasoning. Can you spot what is wrong and reword the premises to show that the conclusion does not follow? Try to make as few changes as possible.

1.
Interesting school books are rare.
Rare books are expensive.
Therefore, interesting school books are expensive.

2.
A noisy child is a headache.
Aspirin makes a headache go away.
Therefore, aspirin makes a noisy child go away.

3.
To end up in Cincinnati you need to go right.
To go right is to be morally virtuous.
Therefore, to end up in Cincinnati you need to be morally virtuous.

Technically, to go *right* as in turning right and to go *right* as in to do what's right are different words that have the same form. More loosely and broadly, however, we talk about using the same word to express different meanings in different contexts. A simple way of ensuring that students are aware of the fact that meaning can vary with use is to provide them with exercises in which the same word is used in contexts where it has different connotations. You can use them as a warm-up for a lesson by choosing a key word relating to its subject matter.

Warm-up Exercise: "Wrong"

Join each sentence to the word on the right that best expresses the meaning of "wrong" in that sentence.

1. Something is *wrong* with the television.	*unjust*
2. Tommy's answers in math are often *wrong*.	*injury*
3. It is *wrong* to jail an innocent person.	*unsuitable*
4. This hairdo is *wrong* for me.	*unethical*
5. I did you no *wrong*.	*incorrect*
6. Torturing animals is *wrong*.	*faulty*

Vagueness

Teachers are all too familiar with students responding vaguely. Sometimes it arises because they lack the detailed knowledge needed to say something more definite and at other times from a lack of understanding. Thus, a student who says that the American Revolutionary War happened centuries ago almost certainly cannot provide its dates, just as the student who reckons that equations are a whole heap of numbers together with an equal sign probably can't more adequately define them.

Sometimes we can tackle vagueness by insisting that students provide facts and figures or learn definitions, but that cannot be expected to do all the work. Consider the facile use of complex concepts. Suppose a student says that the Revolutionary War shows America to have been founded on the value of freedom. While details of the historical record are obviously needed to back up this claim, the concept of freedom is multifaceted, and its meaning is not given simply by citing historical data. It needs to be shown that the evidence cited satisfies the criteria for the application of the concept.

Reference to criteria is one way in which students can sharpen their judgments by subjecting them to clearly defined yardsticks. Vagueness can also be addressed by calling for examples. Examples are one way of moving beyond sweeping statements and vague generalizations. A student who suggests that many of our cities have grown too large, for instance, might be called upon to provide examples and explain why they support that judgment. Similarly, students can often attain greater precision by drawing distinctions. Is the student who says that many cities have grown too large referring to their population or geographical area?

As the mention of examples, distinctions, and criteria indicates, the thinker's toolkit provides many devices for combating vagueness. Relevant examples provide concrete cases of what otherwise may be nebulous claims. Pertinent distinctions bring greater definition to what is being talked about. The meaning of notions becomes clearer when the criteria for their application are revealed. The main strategy for combating vagueness, therefore, is to encourage students to deal with it by using the tools at their disposal.

EXERCISES AND ACTIVITIES

Classification and Division

Exercise: The Same Kind of Thing

The following pairs are things of the same kind. Can you name them?

1. Cups and mugs
2. Knives and forks

3. Sneakers and sandals
4. Buttons and zips
5. Carrots and potatoes
6. Mushrooms and toadstools
7. Gold and silver
8. Snow and ice

Activity: Which Goes with What?

Tiger   Eagle   Alligator   Dolphin   Shrimp   Camel   Penguin
Sheep   Whale   Buffalo   Shark   Peacock   Crab   Seal
Elephant

1. Find clip art images of the animals listed above and make sufficient sets of them so that groups of three or four children can each be given a set. Cut them up to separate the animals and place the sets in envelopes.
2. Divide the class and distribute the envelopes.
3. Tell the class that they are to separate their animals into groups. Explain that they can have as many groups as they like, except that one animal all by itself is not a group of animals. Also tell them that they will need to be able to explain why the animals are in a group using the word "because."
4. After the students have finished dividing their animals, have one or more groups explain their scheme.
5. Allow the class to question any placement or grouping that they think does not work and for the group to reply.
6. Have the groups glue their animals onto sheets of paper and help them to label each group in writing.

Activities of this sort can be constructed for all manner of general categories, as in the following illustrations for foodstuffs and vehicles, using the same procedure.

Activity: Classifying Foodstuffs

apples   potatoes   grapes   hamburgers   fries   pizza   steak
peas   oranges   bread   butter   milk   coffee   soda   beans
yogurt

Activity: Classifying Vehicles

cars   bicycles   motorbikes   planes   helicopters   sailboats   submarines
canoes   rowboats   spaceships   rockets   remote-control cars
skateboard   drones

With appropriate modification, the same kind of activity is also suitable for the later elementary years. Once older students are familiar with collaborative inquiry, you can have each group discuss its results with another group and then end with a brief class discussion of any problems or difficulties encountered in coming up with a solution. Here is an example of the activity for that age group.

Activity: Dividing Things Up

Below is a list of things that are associated with a big city. Your task is to divide them into groups of at least three things and to provide a name or description for each group. Make sure that you leave nothing out and that no item looks like it belongs in more than one group.

skyscrapers   taxi cabs   airports   crowds   downtown
train stations   buses   hotels   helipads   parks   department stores
suburbs   motorways   traffic jams museums

By the time they reach the secondary level, students are much more able to successively divide things up so as to produce classification schemes in tree structures and the like. In the later years of elementary years, however, you can begin to make them familiar with these more complicated cases of classification and division, by giving them appropriate classification schemes and having students work out relationships within them. Family trees provide an obvious example.

Exercise: Family Relationships

Look at the family tree of Homer and Marge Simpson. Homer's parents are Abraham and Mona and he has a brother by the name of Herb. Marge's parents, Clancy and Jackie, had two other daughters, Patty and Selma. After Homer and Marge got together, they had Bart, Lisa, and Maggie. Selma also has a child called Ling.

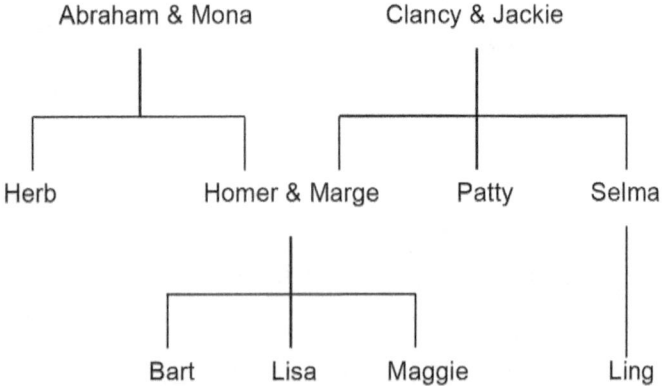

Can you identify the following people?

1. Lisa's father's brother's nephew is _____
2. Clancy's grandson's uncle's father is _____
3. Patty's sister's husband's mother's husband is _____
4. Ling's mother's sister's husband's mother is _____
5. Maggie's sister's uncle's brother's son is _____
6. Ling's cousin's cousin is _____

Constructing a multilayered classification scheme is a surprisingly challenging task. As with the more elementary activities involving division set out above, it is best carried out in small groups. That allows for critical discussion of alternative suggestions to arrive at a resolution, as well as an appreciation of the strengths and weaknesses of different attempts when the students come to look at each other's work as a class. Here are a couple of more complex versions of the earlier activities that are suitable for secondary students.

Activity: Types of Household Furniture

Divide the items listed below into groups according to their normal use. When the items in a group serve related but somewhat different functions, they may need to be divided a second time.

bed   dining chair   desk   dining table   lounge chair   wardrobe
cupboard   bookshelf   coffee table   stool

Activity: Forms of Animal Locomotion

Animal locomotion comes in many forms, some of which are listed below. Arrange them within an inverted treelike structure, with "Animal locomotion" at the top and lines running down to your own descriptions of the broader categories of locomotion into which those listed might be divided. Then run lines down from these categories for each of the items that fall under them. Finally, at the end of each branch, identify at least one kind of animal that uses that form of locomotion.

crawling   jumping   flying   slithering   hopping   running
swimming   gliding   soaring   walking   paddling   leaping
galloping   climbing

Conceptual Opposition

Exercise: Opposites or Not Opposites?

Which of the following are opposites? Where they are not opposites, can you say what the opposite would be and provide an example to prove that they are not opposites.

Poor/Not poor
Acceptable/Not acceptable
Friendly/Not Friendly
Old/Not old
Broken/Not broken
Skinny/Not skinny

Warm-up Activity: Natural

Sort out the words below into those that belong with "natural" and those that go with "not natural." If you aren't certain about a word, then place it under the question mark.

Natural	?	Not Natural

innate   artificial   instinctive   man-made   synthetic   cultivated
unaffected   imitation   genuine   unprocessed   spontaneous

Warm-up Activity: Power

Sort out the words below into those that belong with "having power" and those that go with "lacking power." If you aren't certain about a word, then place it under the question mark.

Having Power	?	Lacking Power

authority   strong   conquered   controlled   govern   influence
dominated   dependent   might   command   ruled   supreme
weak   forceful

With a little effort and ingenuity, you can dramatize such exercises and activities by placing them in a setting that appeals to the imagination. In the middle elementary school exercise below, what would have been a word list is replaced with scenes from an imagined world, and in the activity that follows it, oppositions are used as a basis for story writing.

Exercise: Topsy-Turvy World

In Topsy-Turvy World, things are the opposite of what happens here. Which of the three words best captures the way things are in Topsy-Turvy World?

1. When the sun comes up, it becomes (warm, dark, or colorful).
2. Milk is (colorful, creamy, or black).
3. Skyscrapers are (short, big, or narrow).
4. Water is (thick, cold, or dry).

Activity: Contrasting Characters

Introduce a sense of drama into story writing by means of strong contrasts. Have students write down opposites alongside the words below and then include as many of these contrasts as they can in a story.

Hero/
Wealthy/
Deceitful/
Ugly/
Cruel/
Violent/
Gloomy/
Shabby/
Deserted/

Dichotomous Division

Exercise: Countries and Not Countries

Things that belong to a group share a feature or features that other things lack. Of the things mentioned below, some are countries, while the others are not countries. Start with this and then continue to successively divide up the rest into groups in the same manner until you have run out of categories and covered everything in the list.

New York   Statue of Liberty   London   Ireland   Mount Rushmore
Washington Monument   England   New Zealand   Eiffel Tower
Rome   Hawaii   Empire State Building

Exercise: Classifying Geographical Kinds

Various kinds of things that are found in physical geography are listed below. Some are land masses while others are not. Start by dividing the land masses from everything that is not a land mass and then continue to divide up the rest in the same manner until you have run out of categories and covered everything in the list.

Mountains   Rivers   Lakes   Hills   Moors   Valleys   Oceans
Streams   Islands   Continents   Seas   Bays   Volcanos
Reefs   Prairies

Exercise: Dichotomous Division

Various things that we wear are listed below. Some are footwear while the rest are not. Start by dividing footwear from non-footwear and then continue to divide up the rest of the items in the same manner until you have run out of categories and covered everything in the list.

Shoes   Socks   Dresses   Mittens   Jeans   Caps   Shirts
Coats   Sandals Belts   Hats   Stockings   Pajamas   Slippers
Skirts

Activity: Twenty Questions

The old parlor game Twenty Questions depends on dichotomous division, in which participants successively ask whether a secretly chosen object has a certain feature or not, whittling down the possibilities in an attempt to identify it.

1. Ask for a volunteer to think of an object and quietly tell the teacher.
2. Have the rest of the class then try to identify the object by asking questions that have either a "Yes" or a "No" answer. (Choose the questioner from those who have their hands up, keeping track of the number of questions that have been asked.)
3. After any answer, a student who thinks they know the correct answer can raise both hands and have the opportunity to guess—but they only get to guess once in the game.
4. If no one can guess after twenty questions, have the volunteer reveal the identity of the object to the class.

Distinctions

Don't forget that when teaching students to make distinctions, it is useful have them try to specify the most restrictive general kind that the things in question have in common before they look for what distinguishes them from one another as things of that kind.

Exercise: Making Distinctions

How are the following pairs similar and how are they different?

1. Pushing and pulling
2. Tapping and slapping
3. Hopping and skipping
4. Sitting and squatting
5. Stretching and straining

Exercise: Making Distinctions

How are the following pairs similar and how are they different?

1. Borrowing and stealing
2. Keeping a secret and lying
3. Forgetting and ignoring
4. Arguing and fighting
5. Teasing and taunting

Exercise: Making Distinctions

How are the following pairs similar and how are they different?

1. Cuts and scratches
2. Scabs and blisters
3. Itches and tickles
4. Stings and hives

Exercise: Making Distinctions

How are the following pairs similar and how are they different?

1. A cause and an effect
2. An event and a process
3. Being organic and being inorganic
4. An acid and a base
5. A sea and a lake
6. Perennial and intermittent

The exercise below distinguishes between different things we associate with care. It is being used as a warm-up for a discussion dealing with the concept of care. The Discussion Plan that follows it picks up on the distinction between doing things with care and caring about them and explores some of their differences. There are other possibilities, of course. For instance, the discussion could have set out to disentangle the positive attitudes and emotions associated with care, such as valuing and liking, from negative ones, like faultfinding and worry. You can pair an exercise and a Discussion Plan in this way for all kinds of topics.

Exercise: Care

Together with your partner, join each sentence to the word on the right that best captures the meaning of *care* as it is used in that sentence.

84   Chapter 3

1. He hasn't a *care* in the world.	*value*
2. Would you *care for* a drink?	*caution*
3. The nurse will *take care* of you.	*be willing*
4. *Take care* what you say.	*worry*
5. Would someone *care* to give me a hand?	*look after*
6. You should exercise *care* when handling poisons.	*watch*
7. I *care about* our friendship.	*like*

Discussion Plan: Care

The following questions explore the distinction between caring about what you are doing and doing something carefully. Ask students for examples to justify what they say where that is appropriate.

1. If you do something carefully, does that mean you must want to do it?
2. If you care about what you are doing, does that mean you must want to do it?
3. If you handle something carefully, does that mean you must value it?
4. If you care about what you are handing, does that mean you must value it?
5. Is doing something carefully the same thing as caring about what you are doing?

Definition

Exercise: Defining Types of Musical Instruments

Construct definitions for the musical instruments listed below by following the example of a piano. First, name the general class of instrument to which it belongs, and then identify the distinguishing feature or features that make it different from other things in that class.

	General kind to which it belongs	*Distinguishing feature(s)*
piano	keyboard instrument	with metal stings struck by hammers
drum		
guitar		
violin		
trombone		

Exercise: Definitions in Geometry

Construct definitions for the geometrical objects below by following the example of a triangle. First, name the general kind to which the object belongs, and then identify the distinguishing feature or features that make it different from other things of that kind.

	General kind to which it belongs	Distinguishing feature(s)
triangle	two-dimensional figure	three straight sides, internal angles equal to 180°
right angle		
circle		
cube		
sphere		

Exercise: Defining Celestial Objects

Construct definitions for the celestial objects below by following the example of Mercury. First, name the general kind to which the object belongs, and then identify the distinguishing feature or features that make it different from other things of that kind.

	General kind to which it belongs	Distinguishing feature(s)
Mercury	planet	with the closest orbit to the Sun
Pluto		
Sun		
Moon		
Orion		

Categorical Comparisons

As a reminder that the operation underlying categorical comparisons is classification, here are some elementary exercises that might equally have been placed under that heading.

Exercise: Making Comparisons

In what way are the following pairs basically alike?

House/Burrow
Fort/Prison
Door/Gate
Staircase/Elevator
Bridge/Ferry

Exercise: Making Comparisons

In what way are the following basically alike?

Summer/Winter
Scarf/Mittens
Raincoats/Umbrellas

Hail/Snow
Tornados/Cyclones

Exercise: Making Comparisons

In what way are the following basically alike?

Puppies/Seedlings
Fur/Overcoats
Kennels/Dollhouses
Barking/Doorbells
Tail wagging/Smiling

We now proceed to more complex categorical comparisons, beginning with classical analogies of the form *A is to B as C is to D*.

Exercise: Analogies

Complete the following analogies and be ready to discuss your answers.

1. *Yes* is to *no* as a tick is to _____.
2. The earth is to the sun as the moon is to _____.
3. A horse is to a cowboy as a plane is to _____.
4. Streets are to highways as brooks are to _____.
5. Buns are to burgers as shells are to _____.

Exercise: Seeing Analogies

In what way are the following pairs alike?

SPRING and FALL/TEENAGE and MIDDLE AGE
MOUNTAINS and VALLEYS/ATTICS and BASEMENTS
WHISPERING and SHOUTING/BREEZES and GALES

Exercise: Seeing Analogies

In what way are the following pairs alike?

3 and 4/TUESDAY and WEDNESDAY
LISTENING and SPEAKING/READING and WRITING
BICYCLES and CARS/PEOPLE and CATS

Exercise: Analogies

Connect each statement about a work of art in the list below that best compares with the statements about people.

The shapes were harsh and jarring.
The whole composition was a jumble.
The colors ran into one another and became muddy.
The portrait was deliberately distorted.
His room is a mess with things strewn everywhere.
She refused to eat a balanced diet.
The rapper kept shouting so loudly it grated on the ears.
Her thoughts went in every direction and she became quite confused.

Exercise: Matching Pairs

Sometimes comparisons between matching pairs lend themselves to more than a simple division. Consider the statement "mountains are to hills as continents are to islands." All four things are geographical forms. Mountains and hills are elevated landforms, but one is larger or more elevated than the other. Similarly, continents and islands are both landmasses, but one is bigger or more extensive than the other. This allows us to set out the comparison in the following way.

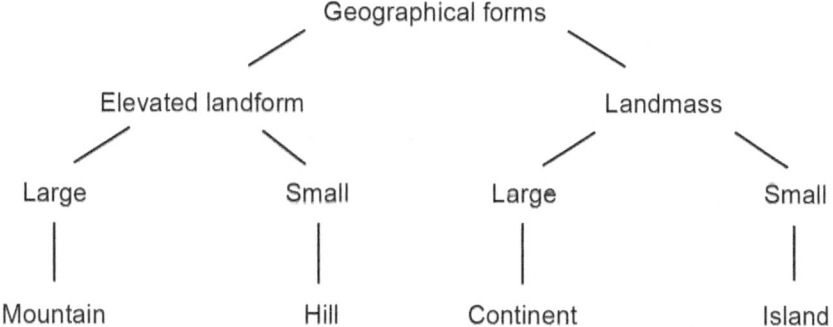

See if you can do the same for the following matching pairs.

1. Eggshell is to tortoiseshell as apple peel is to orange peel.
2. Scissors are to knives as binoculars are to telescopes.
3. Submarines are to cargo ships as subway trains are to trucks.

Comparative Language

Exercise: Making Comparisons

Complete the following sentences by changing the ending of the word in italics to make a comparison. The first example shows you what to do, but exactly what you write for the others is up to you.

1. Today it will be *hot*, but it will be even hotter tomorrow.
2. By early afternoon the traffic was *slow*, but . . . .
3. The skyscrapers in Chicago are *high*, but . . . .
4. The moon is *far* away, but . . . .
5. Coming third in the race was *good*, but . . . .

Exercise: Who Is Making Comparisons?

When are the people below making comparisons?

Mom: Your room will need to be much tidier before grandma comes.
Cindy: But my room is tidy.
Mom: It is the messiest room in the house.
Cindy: Can't I do it later?
Mom: No, you're to do it now.

Exercise: Looking for Comparisons

Words like "faster," "happier," and "kindest" are used to make comparisons, as when someone says that Tom is the fastest runner in the class, that Susanna is happier today than yesterday, or that we have the kindest teacher in the school. Underline all the words that are used to make comparisons in the passage below.

> *Brad loved the circus, especially the clowns. He thought they were the funniest thing in the world. They chased one other around the ring, faster and faster, until they fell over one another in a heap. The short clown was the best juggler. He could juggle six balls. When the tall one tried to do it, he could hardly catch a single ball. You could have done better yourself. The tall clown was shot from a cannon, but was back in the ring quicker than anything. The other one was so short he couldn't climb up into the cannon, even though he tried his hardest. The tiniest little cannon had to be wheeled in for him.*

Ordinal Comparisons

A simple way of representing ordinal comparisons is to use a line to signify the basis of comparison and label it so that it is clear which way the shades or degrees of difference run. This device can provide the basis for warm-up exercises, short activities, and class discussions.

Exercise: Making Comparisons

Procedure

1. Place the comparative terms for the concept at the ends of a line on the board and ask the class to name the concept.
2. Position a word or two along the line and then invite students to supply others that belong somewhere along it. Start with your marker at one end and begin moving along the line, asking the student who suggests a word to stop you when you get to where it belongs.
3. Add the word and then repeat the procedure until the class runs out of words, discussing any uncertainty or disagreements along the way.

Activity: Comparing Size

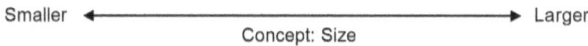

microscopic   tiny   small   smallish   average   biggish
huge   gigantic   gargantuan

Procedure

1. Place a line on the floor of the discussion circle with cards for the comparative terms at the ends and ask the class to name the concept.
2. Have each word from the list on a separate card and hand one out to every pair or threesome in the class, giving them a moment or two to decide roughly where along the line their word belongs.
3. Ask a couple of students to come out and place their words along the line.
4. Now have the rest of the class add their other words, discussing positioning with those nearby as necessary.
5. Once everyone is seated again, read through the words in order, and have the class discuss any remaining disagreement or uncertainty.

Ordinal comparisons aren't limited to simple concepts, of course. They are a way of conceptualizing order in all kinds of domains. An activity of the kind above, for example, could be run with anything that can be ordered in this way and for which students have the requisite vocabulary. Here is an example.

Activity: Comparing Conduct

diabolical   abysmal   flawed   lackluster   passable   reasonable
commendable   excellent   outstanding   angelic

As with many of the operations dealt with in this book, ordinal comparisons can form the basis of a lesson. With appropriate subject matter, what might otherwise have been a warm-up exercise can open up complex topics for discussion. Here are a couple of activities.

Activity: Factors Affecting a Person's Identity

While many factors make up a person's identity, some of them are arguably more significant than others. The following activity provides students with the opportunity to consider the relative significance of a range of such things for a person's identity.

memories   actions   DNA   clothes   gender   parents
education   hobbies   friends   name   face

1. Provide students with the word list.
2. Divide the class into small groups and tell them to order the significance of the things listed in order of importance for a person's identity.
3. Give the groups time to discuss the relative significance of the factors on the list.
4. Have one or two groups present their results to the class.
5. Conduct a class discussion, based on any disagreements or uncertainty with what was presented.

Activity: Use and Abuse of Animals

```
Less                                              More
acceptable                                        acceptable
```

Bullfighting   Battery hens   Hunting elephants for their tusks
Guide dogs for the blind   Using animals to test cosmetics   Using animals for medical research   Killing whales   Horse racing

Procedure

1. Place the labeled line in the center of the discussion circle and then divide the class into groups and give each group a card from those set out above.
2. Give the groups a few minutes to decide roughly where along the line it belongs and why.

3. Ask a group that took their card to belong toward one end of the spectrum to place their card where they think it belongs and to present the reasons for its decision. Record the gist of them with a dot-point or two on the board. (Do not embark upon further discussion at this stage. There will be an opportunity to do so at the end.)
4. Do the same for a group that took their card to belong toward the other end of the spectrum.
5. Have the other groups introduce all the other cases, with reasons to be stated briefly.
6. Open up the order of placement for discussion, intervening when necessary to assist students to uncover any general conditions or considerations that make some cases better or worse than others. Don't forget to record them on the board.

Comparisons of Quality and Quantity

The following exercises ask students to distinguish between qualitative and quantitative comparisons. They are meant for senior secondary students.

Exercise: Comparisons of Quantity and Quality

Is the comparison involved in the following cases one of quality or of quantity?

1. A picture is worth a thousand words.
2. Where ignorance is bliss, 'tis folly to be wise.
3. Kindness, like a boomerang, always returns.
4. Fifty percent of something is better than one hundred percent of nothing.
5. Actions speak louder than words.
6. One should speak little with others and much with oneself.

Exercise: Comparisons of Quantity and Quality

In each of the following cases, say whether the comparison involved is one of quality or of quantity.

1. She was as cool as a cucumber.
2. Keep your friends close, but your enemies closer.
3. Like father, like son.
4. Kindness, like grain, increases by sowing.
5. A stitch in time saves nine.
6. Cleanliness is next to godliness.

Examining the Basis of Comparisons

Exercise: Examining Comparisons

Together with a partner, try to identify the basis of comparison in the cases below. Be prepared for further discussion with the rest of the class.

1. His anger arose like a storm.
2. The children lay in their sleeping bags like sardines in a can.
3. She had a complexion like peaches and cream.
4. They descended the mineshaft as into a mystery.

Exercise: Examining Comparisons

Saying that eating is to hunger as drinking is to thirst is to make a comparison. In this case, it is easy to identify the basis of comparison. Both satisfy the need for sustenance. See if you can identify the basis of comparison in the cases below. It may take some discussion.

1. Principals are to schools as captains are to ships.
2. Teachers are to students as gardeners are to plants.
3. Achievement is to hard work as pizza is to cheese.
4. Waking is to falling asleep as remembering is to forgetting.

Exercise: Reasoning with Comparisons

The following people are making a claim based on a comparison between two things. What is the basis of their comparison and how well does it support their claim?

Brad: The Mississippi River passes through more states than the Missouri River and so the Mississippi has got to be longer than it.

Rachel: There must be more water coming over Niagara Falls than any other waterfall in the country. It has the greatest flow rate and its combined width is greater than any of the others.

Naomi: Olympus Mons is the tallest mountain on Mars, but it can't be as tall as Mount Everest, the tallest mountain on earth. After all, Mars is much smaller than the earth.

Mike: When you take a trip up through mountainous country and come back home, you must have gone up just as much as you came down. Otherwise you would end up in the air or under the ground.

Jacinta: You can compare the coastlines of the world's continents to a jigsaw puzzle that all fits together. So, once upon a time they formed one great landmass.

Complex Concepts

When students are ready to tackle complex concepts, it is worth beginning with a discussion of the difficulties they pose and to have an experience of making headway with them.

Discussion Plan: I Know What It Means, but . . . .

1. Do you sometimes know what a word means and yet have difficulty trying to explain what it means? Can you give an example?
2. You know what friendship is, so try to define it. Was that difficult?
3. Why is it sometimes difficult to explain the meaning of familiar words?
4. Let's brainstorm a list of things that you would look for in a friend. What does that tell you about friendship?
5. Can there be different kinds of friendships? What are the ones that come to mind?
6. Is the concept of friendship simple or complicated?

The other thing to begin with in exploring complex concepts is to get students used to searching for the criteria that govern them. Exercises that target criteria provide an effective means of doing this, especially when they lead to discussion or activities that center on those criteria. Here are three examples.

Exercise: What Is a Criterion?

A *criterion* is the basis on which someone makes a judgment. If a sports umpire were to favor one team over another, that wouldn't be fair. He should treat both teams the same. To say that fairness demands equal treatment is to make equal treatment the *criterion* of fairness in this case. The people below each rely on a different criterion for judging that something either is or is not fair. Can you say what they are? Be ready to discuss what you think with the class.

Rebecca: Why does Mandy always get to go first? That isn't fair.
Amanda: Dianne did more work than anyone else. It's only fair that she should get the prize.
Jasper: It isn't fair to punish me for hitting Donald. He started it.
Walt: It's fair enough for Bobby to be captain. That's what most kids want.

Exercise: Common Criteria of Friendship

While friendships vary a great deal, they tend to share some common features. The people below are not behaving like friends. See whether you can identify the features of friendship that they fail to display.

1. Whenever Jordan meets up with Liam they get into a fight.
2. Tiffany thinks that Sam is a little liar.
3. Max can never figure out where Nathan is coming from.
4. Steve and Damien have very little in common.
5. Rebecca often thinks about Mia, but Mia hardly ever thinks about her.

Exercise: Criteria of Moral Judgment

People often rely on the consequences of conduct as their criterion of moral judgment. Which of the people below are doing that? Where they are not, what other kinds of criteria are they relying on?

Mom: So long as you end up being happy with what you do, it's all that matters.
Sam: I didn't mean any harm.
Verity: Capital punishment is wrong. It's against the sixth commandment.
Rupert: If it means that nobody is worse off, where's the harm in it?
Amy: I can see the benefits of what you're proposing, but it doesn't feel right to me.
Dad: I wouldn't be blaming you if you hadn't left things lying about for someone to trip over.

Let us recall the use of various kinds of cases in conceptual exploration. *Paradigm cases* are ones that indisputably fall under the concept in question. They satisfy all the necessary criteria. *Borderline cases* have some relevant features, but in other ways are questionable. They help to identify reasons for inclusion or exclusion. *Contrary cases* are ones that definitely do not fall under the concept. They fail to satisfy necessary criteria, or whatever criteria they do satisfy are clearly not sufficient for the concept to be applied to them.[4]

While a well-chosen borderline or contrary case can be a fruitful way of flushing out criteria, a mixture of paradigm, borderline, and contrary cases is generally the most effective. Students can often come up with the latter themselves in the form of a counterexample to some proposed criterion. All three kinds of cases (together with the search for a counterexample) are included in the following Discussion Plan.

Discussion Plan: What Makes Something a Work of Art?

1. Leonardo da Vinci's painting of the *Mona Lisa* is a famous work of art. What makes it a work of art?
2. Could a painting made by an elephant be a work of art?

3. Could an uncontrollable sneeze be a work of art? If not, why not?
4. Suppose someone said that anything produced by an artist is art. Can anyone think of something that might be produced by an artist but isn't art?

There is no one strategy that you have to follow. Where a concept applies to a range of cases, it can be quite effective to stick to them in order to bring out its characteristics. The following examples are of that kind, the first one focusing on common characteristics and the second varying ones.

Discussion Plan: Community

1. Some people live in rural communities. What makes them communities?
2. Can you give an example of an ethnic community? What makes it a community?
3. What would be an example of a religious community? What makes it a community?
4. When people talk about the scientific community, what do they mean?
5. When people talk about the global community, what do they mean?
6. What is a community?

Discussion Plan: What Makes a Rule Fair?

Discuss the following questions, calling for examples and exploring them where that is appropriate.

1. Are rules sometimes fair because they treat everyone alike?
2. Can a rule be fair in distinguishing between people according to their needs?
3. Could a rule be fair because it aims at the overall happiness of those to whom it applies?
4. Can rules be fair because they are accepted by the vast majority of people?
5. Might a rule be fair in favoring a group that was discriminated against in the past?

While a Discussion Plan is one way to go, you can often cover much the same ground by means of an activity. This may be more attractive to students, especially when it involves consideration of scenarios that make the conceptual content more concrete and familiar. Let's do that for rules and fairness, so as to compare this approach with the use of a Discussion Plan in the illustration above.

Activity: Is That Rule Fair?

1. Emma thinks that the school rules aren't fair because they treat everyone alike when students are all different.
2. My math teacher makes it a rule to spend a lot of time helping those kids who need more help.
3. Mia hates the novel that Mr. Butler set this term, but it was one the class was happiest with and he was ruled by that.
4. Benjamin's group makes it a rule to always do what the majority wants.
5. Liam reckons that there should be a rule to favor kids who keep missing out.

You can also arrange for discussion as a follow-up to an exercise. Consider the following exercise that deals with the use of the word "free" in various contexts, for example.

Warm-up Exercise: Free

Join the sentence on the left to the word on the right that best replaces the word *free* in that sentence.

1. The doctor is *free* to see you now.	*release*
2. Buy one and get another one absolutely *free*.	*exempt*
3. You may *free* the prisoner.	*unblock*
4. You are not *free* to do whatever you want.	*available*
5. He used a plunger to *free* the drain.	*without charge*
6. Is this seat *free*?	*able*
7. These goods are no longer *free* from tax.	*allowed*

Having completed the exercise as a warm-up, the lesson can move on to a Discussion Plan which explores the same material.

Discussion Plan: Free

1. Is being free in the sense of being without charge completely different from the other cases presented in the exercise? (How about being tax exempt?)
2. Is unblocking a drain in any way like releasing a prisoner? What about unblocking and releasing more generally?
3. Is there any similarity between the doctor being free to see you and a seat being available? (Both are at someone's disposal.)
4. Finish by having students go through the cases trying to redescribe them using the word *allowed*, as in, "You are allowed to see the doctor now" and "You may allow the prisoner to go."

Alternatively, we can follow the warm-up with an activity based on a set of scenarios that appeal to various criteria related to freedom. Trying to decide whether and in what sense the scenarios are examples of freedom, and where and why they may be problematic, will reveal many of the criteria that govern the concept. The following can be carried out in any of the ways set out for similar activities.

Activity: Freedom

Free	?	Not Free

1. Di's mother doesn't allow her to play with other children after school.
2. Jack's parents allow him to do whatever he likes.
3. Sandra gets to choose all her own clothes.
4. Nick wants a mountain bike but his parents can't afford one.
5. Elias has a wonderful imagination.
6. In Mr. Cooper's class, students are encouraged to express their opinions.
7. Michelle managed to miss sport for a month because her leg was in plaster.
8. Boris is in jail.

We can do the same with any complex concept. Earlier we had an exercise devoted to the criteria of friendship. Friendship is important to us all, but what is involved in being a friend—let alone a good friend or someone's best friend—is not immediately obvious, as discussion of the following scenarios will reveal.

Activity: Are They Acting Like Friends?

Acting Like a Friend	?	Not Acting Like a Friend

1. Tony and Rob hang around together, but they continually fight with one another.
2. Felicity is forever teasing Rosa. One day when Rosa complained, Felicity said that she shouldn't let little things bug her.
3. Jamal and Pham are said to be friends, but Jamal seldom picks Pham to be on his team in sport.
4. Beth says that she is Trudy's friend, but she bosses her about.
5. Sandy thinks of Alex as a friend, but she knows that sometimes he lies to her.
6. Martin and Ariel were friends, but when Martin started doing drugs, Ariel dobbed him in.

Here is one more exercise followed by an activity that explores a complex concept: the role of punishment in concept of justice. The warm-up exercise involves having students work together, whether in pairs or as a class, to decide which words belong with "Just" and which ones with "Not just." The activity that follows it can be handled in the usual way.

Exercise: Words Having to Do with Justice

Just	?	Not Just

impartial	undeserved	evenhanded		excessive	merited
biased	discriminatory	fair	prejudiced	fitting	one-sided

Activity: Punishment and the Concept of Justice

Just	?	Not Just

1. Bruno was expelled for being a bully so that other students wouldn't have to put up with him.
2. The lie that Mary told about Alex hurt him badly, but being found out was sufficient to stop Mary doing it again and so that was punishment enough.
3. Riana's punishment for humiliating Sandra in front of her classmates was to be stood before the class and humiliated.
4. Although Jesse admitted cheating, he was let off because he showed genuine remorse.
5. Indira washed out her little brother Ari's mouth with soap because he spoke rudely to her.

Nearly all of the illustrations of working with complex concepts have dealt with largely social conceptions of fairness, freedom, and friendship. Let's end with a completely different concept—the concept of *mind*. It has been much discussed in philosophy, but also relates to psychology and what is now called cognitive science. While this makes it sound like a formidable concept for secondary school students, there is no reason why they could not tackle it quite well in their own terms.

Exercise and Activity: Mind

Mind	?	No Mind

- A chess-playing computer program
- A computer brain that works just like a human brain
- A person with an electronic brain
- A person who cannot think at all

- Someone without any memory
- A person who is in a sound and dreamless sleep
- A mosquito
- A nation

Here is the procedure to follow:

1. Make copies of the headings and the list above for each group of three or four students. Also have them on the board.
2. Explain that the question mark card means either that you aren't certain whether something has a mind or that there is disagreement about the matter.
3. Divide the class into groups and give each group a copy of the worksheet.
4. Give the groups around ten minutes or so to discuss whether or not each of the things named have a mind, with reasons for their responses. If the members of the group cannot agree, they will need to be able to explain the reason for their disagreement.
5. Reassemble the class and invite a group to say that something either does or does not have a mind and to give its reasons. Dot-point their main reason or reasons alongside that item on the board.
6. If other members of the class dispute what was said, open the matter up for a brief discussion. Record any additional points on the board.
7. Proceed in the same way with the other cases, leaving any cases where there was widespread uncertainty or disagreement until last.
8. Go back over the results on the board assisting the class to extract the main criteria that they have employed for saying that something has a mind.

Clarification

Exercise: Let's Clear That Up

The statements below suggest something that the speaker did not intend. Work with your partner to rewrite the statements so as to make the intention clear, making as few changes as possible.

1. Mix the flour and butter together with your hands until they become crumbly.
2. A golfer who yesterday hit his ball into the onlookers has today made a hole in one.
3. Mrs. McFadden took her dog Fifi for a walk in her curlers.
4. Shortages in the building trade are making bricklayers turn to concrete.
5. The murderer was given a life sentence in the poisoned pencil case.

Exercise: That's Not What I Mean

The speakers below might be taken to suggest something that they did not mean. Work with your partner to rewrite the sentences with as few changes as possible so as to make their intention clear.

1. Grandmas make great weekend roasts.
2. The lion attacked the zookeeper with a whip.
3. At his retrial, the murderer was sentenced to die for a second time.
4. We need to cut through the red tape that is holding up the new bridge.
5. Many of the poor people in the fishing villages live on water.

Exercise: That Doesn't Follow!

Something has gone wrong in the following examples of reasoning. Making as little change as possible, reword the first premise to show that the conclusion does not follow.

1.
This ping-pong ball is light.
Light is nothing but electromagnetic radiation.
Therefore, this ping-pong ball is nothing but electromagnetic radiation.
2.
Your plan is sound.
Sound is an audible waveform.
Therefore, your plan is an audible waveform.
3.
They could see that his argument had force.
Force is something that we learn about in physics.
Therefore, they could see that his argument had something that we learn about in physics.

Warm-up Exercise: Good

Join each sentence to the word on the right that best expresses the meaning of "good" in that sentence.

Everyone had a *good* time.	talented
Give your teeth a *good* brushing.	worthy
No *good* will come from it.	well-behaved
She gave her money to a *good* cause.	enjoyable
He is a very *good* musician.	benefit
Show grandma how *good* you can be.	thorough

Warm-up Exercise: Think

Join each sentence to the word on the right that best expresses the meaning of the word or words in italics in that sentence.

The world is stranger than you *think*.	reflect
Chloe didn't know what to *think*.	imagine
I *don't think* that he did it.	recall
Think on what you have done.	doubt
Justin couldn't *think of* the answer.	concentrate
Kayla was so upset, she couldn't *think*.	believe

Warm-up Exercise: Courage

Many words are associated with courage. Join each sentence to the word on the right that best expresses what is meant by referring to courage in that sentence.

It takes *courage* to say a thing like that.	urge
We *encourage* you to try harder.	promote
Take *courage*! We are sure to be rescued.	guts
The doctor said that her test results were quite *encouraging*.	brave
Liquor shops should not *encourage* heavy drinking.	heart
He received the Medal of Honor for being very *courageous*.	reassuring

NOTES

1. A useful source for this notion in Piaget is his *Genetic Epistemology* (New York: Columbia University Press, 1970).

2. While we are following standard grammatical usage, it is somewhat unfortunate that we use the term "comparative" to identify this class of comparisons, given that categorical systems also involve comparisons.

3. Here again we need to bear in mind that comparisons do not always follow this pattern. If Andy is the *same* height as Mandy, for instance, then Mandy is the *same* height as Andy, and if Andy is *different* in height from Mandy, then Mandy is a *different* height from Andy. Here the relationship expressed is the same in both directions. Even so, there is a compelling argument for setting such cases aside in discussing comparative operations. To say that two things are exactly alike in some respect is to put them in the same class. To say simply that they are unalike in some respect is to categorize them differently. Properly speaking, therefore, these are categorical rather than comparative judgments.

4. By the way, students should be familiar with necessary and sufficient conditions by the time they are in the junior secondary school. We will deal with them in chapter 4.

Chapter 4

Reasoning

> If logic itself is created rather than bring inborn, it follows that the first task of education is to form reasoning.
>
> Jean Piaget

We need to pay attention to reasoning in school education. Muddle-headedness, fallacious reasoning, jumping to conclusions, failing to infer consequences—such things are all too common in daily life. They can be costly, even dangerous. By contrast, those who learn to reason well are better able to work things out for themselves and make good decisions. They are more inclined to examine what is put before them and to think things through. The same is true in the classroom. Students who become used to reasoning about subject matter are less likely to simply regurgitate what they are given and better able to see its implications.

There is no better way of developing students' powers of reasoning than to engage them in collaborative inquiry-based learning. By working together in this way, they are constantly drawing out the implications of one another's suggestions in order to evaluate them. They look to see whether someone's claim makes questionable assumptions, or has implications that run contrary to what they know. They compare the implications of one suggestion with those arising from others with which it competes. All these things develop their ability to reason.

THE LANGUAGE OF REASONING

In terms of language use, reasoning has to do with a relation between statements, in which one or more statements, called the *premises*, are said to imply or justify another statement, referred to as the *conclusion*. An important early step in teaching reasoning is to train students to look out for words that indicate its occurrence. The following is a list of some common indicator words:

Premise indicators

- because
- if
- since
- given that
- inasmuch as
- on account of

Conclusion indicators

- therefore
- then
- hence
- it follows that
- so
- consequently

These words are also used in other ways, of course. In "You have *given that* excuse *so* often" and "*It follows that* path," for instance, none of the italicized words are reasoning indicators. Indicator words may also be merely implicit. An implicit "so" or "therefore" connects a pair of sentences like "I don't have enough ice-creams for everyone. Someone will have to miss out" and there is a tacit "because" in "Don't do it. You'll get into trouble."

In looking out for indicator words, therefore, students need to be mindful of whether they are being explicitly or implicitly used to justify a statement or to draw a conclusion. When they adopt that frame of mind, they will quickly uncover the occurrence of reasoning. This doesn't mean that it is always easy to see exactly how the reasoning is meant to go. Proficiency in the analysis of reasoning requires practice.

Of all the words in the list, it is best to start with "because" and "therefore." Some teachers of young children say that they prefer to use the word "so" instead of "therefore" to introduce inference-making, but "so" has *so* many other uses—isn't that *so*? Whereas "therefore" is specifically designed for that purpose. Once students are familiar with the operations that these words help them to perform, other words from the above list and their variants can be introduced when it is appropriate.

JUSTIFICATION AND INFERENCE

In talking about reasoning, we need to distinguish between related but importantly distinct cognitive operations. From a logical point of view, we *give reasons* in order to justify some statement, but we *reason* in order to infer a conclusion. Justification and inference are obviously different things and yet they are closely related. They are the inverse of one another. Here is a simple example to illustrate:

Justification: Whales must be warm-blooded *because* whales are mammals.
Inference: Whales are mammals. *Therefore*, whales must be warm-blooded.

Justification—or more precisely, *logical justification*—and inference are the basic operations of reasoning.[1]

The give-and-take of reasons and the drawing of inferences constitute a large part of the collaborative inquiry process. We use logical justification when we give reasons to support a suggestion and employ inference to see where a suggestion or the facts before us may lead. Regardless of whether we use terms like "justification" and "inference" with younger students, we need to focus upon these operations from the beginning. This includes giving clear instructions, such as "give a reason" and "draw a conclusion," as well as introducing and emphasizing the word "because" to give a reason and "therefore" to indicate that an inference is being drawn.

In terms of language use, we may say that logical justification deals with logical relations between *statements*, where we use one or more statements to support another statement. From a cognitive point of view, however, we can say that logical justification deals with the relationship between *judgments*, where one or more judgments is used to justify another judgment. The same can be said for inference. Linguistically, it deals with statements that can be inferred from other statements, whereas cognitively it involves judgments made on the basis of other judgments.

Engaging students in logical justification and inference-making during collaborative inquiry involves a metacognitive shift that focuses attention on thinking. Rather than devoting all their attention to information that is put to them, students are learning to attend to logical relationships between their judgments and between the statements that they make. We may liken this to bifocal vision. By keeping one eye on the subject matter and the other eye on the operations they employ in thinking about it, they are able to see things in depth.

Here are a couple of elementary school exercises that are designed to draw attention to these operations.

Exercise: Making Inferences

Below there are four pairs of statements where the word "therefore" can be used to show that one statement follows from the other. Find the pairs and then put them together in the right order, using "therefore" to connect them.

- Robert is ten.
- Jessica is taller than Jasmin, but shorter than Robert.
- Jasmin was on top.
- Robert is twice as old as Jasmin, who is only five.
- Jasmin is the lightest of the three.
- Jessica is lighter than Robert, but heavier than Jasmin.
- Robert is the tallest of the three.
- Jasmin sat on Jessica's shoulders, while Jessica sat on Robert's shoulders.

Exercise: Justifying Beliefs and Opinions

The people below are attempting to justify a belief or opinion by giving reasons. In each case, state the belief or opinion involved and then connect it with the reason or reasons provided, using the word "because."

1. Angela insisted that a tomato is a fruit and not a vegetable, as it develops from a flower.
2. Robert wondered whether spiders are insects, but Naomi said that they aren't. She said that spiders have eight legs, while insects have six.
3. Sam and Andy were talking about the difference between bees and flies. Andy said that bee's wings are different from fly's wings. He claimed that bees have two sets of wings, while flies have only one. Sam added that bees also fold their wings into their bodies when they are at rest, whereas flies spread them out.

Exercises of this kind provide a way of introducing justification and inference, but need to be followed up by asking students to perform these operations when that is appropriate during discussion. Questions such as "Why is that?" and "Why do you think so?" are requests for logical justification, just as "What does that imply?" and "What conclusion can we draw?" call for inference. They should be asked whenever a suggestion is in need of support or students need to examine the implications of what is said.

As we saw earlier, logical justification and inference are related operations, which are the *inverse* of one another. Once students are familiar with the two operations, it is time to make them aware of the connection between the two. With practice, they will be able to move backward and forward between justification and inference and this will be a great leap forward in their capacity to reason and inquire.

You can use examples like the one about whales to make students aware of this connection and follow that up with exercises to establish proficiency, while exploiting opportunities to move between justification and inference in discussion and written work. Here are a couple of exercises to give students practice. The first one is pitched at middle elementary school, while the second is designed for junior secondary. Notice that "because" and "therefore" are not always present in the secondary exercise, requiring students to look for other clues to determine what Mickey and Michaela are doing.

Exercise: Giving Reasons and Drawing Conclusions

In each case below, say whether Bella and Buddy are giving a reason or drawing a conclusion? If they are giving a reason, then turn around what they have said and make it into drawing a conclusion using "therefore." Similarly, if they are drawing a conclusion, then turn around what they have said and make it into giving a reason using "because."

Bella: It is no fun being a stray dog because no one wants to pat a stray dog.
Buddy: I have to guard the house. Therefore, I bark at people passing by.
Bella: I sit when I am told because I am an obedient dog.
Buddy: I get to play with my friends in the park. Therefore, I like to go to the park.

Exercise: Justification and Inference

In each case below, say whether Mickey and Michaela are justifying a claim or drawing an inference. If they are engaged in justification, reverse what they have said, turning it into an inference using "therefore." Similarly, if they are drawing an inference, then reverse what they have said and turn it into supplying a justification using "because."

Mickey: There is no such thing as a number, since numbers are nowhere to be found.
Michaela: There must be numbers. We use them to make calculations.

Mickey: There is no such thing as being exactly "the same" because no two things are exactly alike.

Michaela: Given that 4/8 and 2/4 both come to 1/2, it follows that they are exactly the same.

In an elementary school setting, it is a good idea to pin up a pair of cards (one with *BECAUSE* and the other with *THEREFORE*) when you teach these operations, emphasize their use, or display associated written work. While secondary students will be familiar with ∴ as shorthand for "therefore," it is worth pointing out that ∵ is shorthand for "because," making one symbol the inverse of the other. The folks who devised that arrangement knew what they were doing!

CONDITIONAL REASONING

The most common form for introducing inference takes us from what we know to be true, or from what we believe to be so, to what we are trying to establish. We argue that *since* such and such is the case, *then* so-and-so must be (or is likely to be) the case as well. When we are inquiring into suggestions, however, we are not dealing with "since" but with "if." Here we reason that *if* such and such is (or were) the case, *then* so-and-so will be, or is likely to be (or would be, or would likely be) so as well. In such cases we can be said to reason *conditionally*.

The if-clause of a conditional is called the "antecedent" and the then-clause is called the "consequent." When introducing the conditional to children in the early years of school, however, we can call the antecedent the "if-bit" and the consequent the "then-bit." Children as young as six or seven have no difficulty with this.

No matter what their age, students will be familiar with the "if . . . then . . ." construction from everyday use.

Naomi: *If* I get into trouble at school, *then* my mum will throw a fit.
Brian: Well, *if* I were you, *then* I would apologize to Ms. McDonald before she phones your mum.

It has many variations, including implicit terms and conditions, the substitution for "if" or "then" of logically equivalent expressions, as well as reversal in the order of the clauses.

Naomi: *If* she phones my mother, [*then*] I'm going to be grounded for a week.

Brian: [*If* you're going to be grounded for a week] *Then* go and apologize.
Naomi: *Whenever* I get into trouble at school, I end up grounded.
Brian: It's my dad who throws a fit, *if* I get into trouble.

A wide array of relationships can be expressed by means of the conditional, including conceptual, logical, causal, and mathematical relationships.

- If someone is a centenarian, then they are at least one hundred years old. (*conceptual*)
- If all men are mortal and Socrates is a man, then Socrates is mortal. (*logical*)
- If you heat water at sea level to 212° Fahrenheit, then it will boil. (*causal*)
- If you multiply 6 by 8 and divide by 2, then you get 24. (*mathematical*)

Conditionals are commonly used to express an extensive range of human acts, such as predicting, planning, promising, warning, and bargaining.

- If it keeps on raining like this, then we will have a flood. (*predicting*)
- If I keep moving my queen forward, then I can control the center of the board. (*planning*)
- If you get all your homework done, then I will take you to the beach. (*promising*)
- If you don't clean up your room, then you won't get your pocket money. (*warning*)
- If you give me that Darth Vader card, then you can have my Luke Skywalker. (*bargaining*)

You can begin to use the conditional construction for the purposes of inquiry-based teaching by asking questions that invite conditional reasoning. Such questions are themselves typically conditional in form. Here are some common examples:

- If that happens, then what does it cause? (*reasoning about causal consequences*)
- If that is true, then what would follow? (*reasoning about logical consequences*)
- If it had happened (which it didn't), then what would it have shown? (*counterfactual reasoning*)

We need to ask these kinds of questions and encourage students to develop the habit of asking them too. One way we can do this is to introduce related exercises and activities, as well as engaging students in discussion of problems and issues where these kinds of questions naturally come up. Here is an activity and an exercise by way of illustration, one for early childhood education and the other a challenging extension exercise for somewhat older students.

Activity: "If . . . then . . ."

Procedure

1. Introduce the "if . . . then . . ." construction by way of examples, using the terms "if-bit" and "then-bit."
2. Have each student think of an if-bit.
3. Divide the class into two lines facing one another. One will be the *If* group and the other the *Then* group. Place a card with "if" in front of the *If* group and one with "then" in front of the *Then* group.
4. Give a volunteer in the *If* group a large ball and ask that student to start a sentence with their if-bit.
5. Ask students on the *Then* line to think of a then-bit that could be used to complete the sentence. Have them raise their hands so that the volunteer can choose someone and roll the ball to them.
6. Ensure that the student who responds repeats the whole sentence, including the "if" and "then."
7. Have the ball returned to a volunteer in the *If* group and start the process over again with another student, repeating the process several times.
8. Swap the *If* and *Then* groups and continue as before.

Exercise: Reasoning with "If . . . then . . ."

Imagine that each of the pictures shown represent a double-sided card with another picture on the back. The cards have either a cat or a mouse on one side and either a bowl of milk or a piece of cheese on the other. Here is a suggestion about these cards: If card has a cat on one side, then it will have a bowl of milk on the other. Work with your partner to decide which cards you have to turn over in order to see whether that is right. Don't suggest turning over any card that you don't need to turn over and be ready to explain your reasoning.

Suggestion: If a card has a cat on one side, then it has a bowl of milk on the other.

Students should be able to work out why we need to turn over the cat but not the mouse. We need to see whether there is milk on the back of the cat, but the suggestion doesn't say what to expect if you have a mouse. They may have more difficulty with the other cards. To find a cat on the other side of the milk is consistent with the suggestion, but so is finding a mouse. The suggestion doesn't rule out a mouse having milk on the back. While we don't need to turn over the milk, we do need to turn over the cheese. If we found a cat on the other side, then it isn't true that a card with a cat on one side always has a bowl of milk on the other.

DEDUCTIVE REASONING

Deductive reasoning is fuelled by the desire to preserve truth when we reason. Provided that our premises are true, our conclusion is logically guaranteed to be true when we reason deductively, so long as we don't make mistakes along the way. It is the kind of reasoning that we find in math. Mathematical deduction guarantees that its results follow from its inputs provided that we don't make mathematical errors along the way, just as logical deduction guarantees its results provided that we don't make logical mistakes.

In this respect, deductive method is different from the overall method of inquiry. Inquiry does not involve simply deducing results from what we already know. Rather, it employs suggestions that can be put to the test, the results of which help to secure our conclusions if they come through them unscathed.

Even so, deductive reasoning is an indispensable tool in the inquirer's kit. We use deductive reasoning when we draw out the logical consequences of a suggestion, for example, as well as when we argue that a suggestion should be rejected because it has implications that are not consistent with the evidence.

Categorical Forms of Deductive Reasoning

A piece of reasoning from premises to a conclusion is called an *argument*. When we refer to an argument in reasoning, we are not referring to a heated verbal dispute, of course, but to the application of logical operations to statements. A deductive argument is said to be *valid* if, and only if, it is logically impossible for its premises to be true while its conclusion is false. As we will see, validity is not dependent on the subject matter with which an argument deals, but is entirely dependent on what we may call the argument's *form*.

In chapter 3, we dealt with statements that are said to be *categorical*. Reasoning with such categorical statements is an ancient form of argumentation known as the *syllogism*. Syllogistic arguments are based on statements of the following underlying forms, using F and G to stand for terms:

- All F are G.
- No F are G.
- Some F are G.
- Some F are not G.

Even quite young students can get the feel for arguments of this type by working with examples, using premises and conclusions based on familiar material, such as in the following example based on Eric Carle's classic picture book *The Very Hungry Caterpillar*.[2]

Activity: Therefore

1.
All little caterpillars hatch from an egg.
Nothing that hatches from an egg can grow without eating.
Therefore: No little caterpillars can grow without eating.

2.
Some little caterpillars keep on eating all the time.
Nothing that keeps on eating all the time can stop itself from becoming big and fat.
Therefore: Some little caterpillars cannot stop themselves becoming big and fat.

3.
All caterpillars build cocoons.
All creatures that build cocoons develop wings.
Therefore: All caterpillars develop wings.

4.
Some butterflies are beautiful things.
All beautiful things are lovely to look at.
Therefore: Some butterflies are lovely to look at.

Here is the procedure to follow:

1. Make separate cards for each of the premises and conclusions large enough to be read by the class when placed in the middle of the discussion circle.

2. Put the conclusions in a line below one another in the discussion circle, leaving room for students to add the premises alongside.
3. Divide the class into groups, shuffle the premise cards, and hand out one card to each group.
4. Go around the class, having each group read out their card and hold it up so that it can be seen. Ask the students to keep their cards up after they have read them, so that others can continue to see them.
5. As the cards are read out, the students are to be on the lookout for another card that goes with their card, which together entitles them to draw one of the conclusions on the floor.
6. Ask the students to come out and lay their cards alongside the appropriate conclusion.
7. Have the class discuss any conflicts or mistakes that may have arisen.

Having run such an activity with the aid of familiar material, you can employ nonsensical premises and conclusions, while setting out the premises and conclusions in a more formal fashion, to emphasize the argument's form. Then, to really highlight form, try replacing terms with symbols. Here are versions of the same activity that present more challenging follow-ups.

Activity: Therefore
1.
All icky wiggles are creatures with muggy pits.
All creatures with muggy pits are boggle wops.
Therefore: All icky wiggles are boggle wops.
2.
All muddy mites are worry wops.
No worry wops are doodlers.
Therefore: No muddy mites are doodlers.
3.
Some tiny tiddlers are terrible worriers.
No terrible worriers are things to keep in jig jars.
Therefore: Some tiny tiddlers are not things to keep in jig jars.
4.
Some pitters are snipers.
All snipers are creatures that like to biff.
Therefore: Some pitters are creatures that like to biff.

Activity: Therefore

1.

All ♥ are ☻.

All ☻ are Ω.

Therefore: All ♥ are Ω.

2.

All ♠ are ☼.

No ☼ are △.

Therefore: No ♠ are △.

3.

Some Ψ are ♣.

No ♣ are ✷.

Therefore: Some Ψ are not ✷.

4.

Some ♦ are ■.

All ■ are ✿.

Therefore: Some ♦ are ✿.

Checking for Validity Using Venn Diagrams

The most intuitive way to teach students to explore syllogistic arguments is by means of Venn diagrams, which represent relations between categories or classes. Working in this way enables students to connect syllogistic reasoning with categorical forms of conceptualization.

With Venn diagrams we can use a pair of overlapping circles to represent the categories of things that are *F* and things that are *G*. Then we can shade a region to represent it as empty and put an *X* in a region to show that it is not empty. In this way, we can represent each of the above four forms of categorical statements as shown.

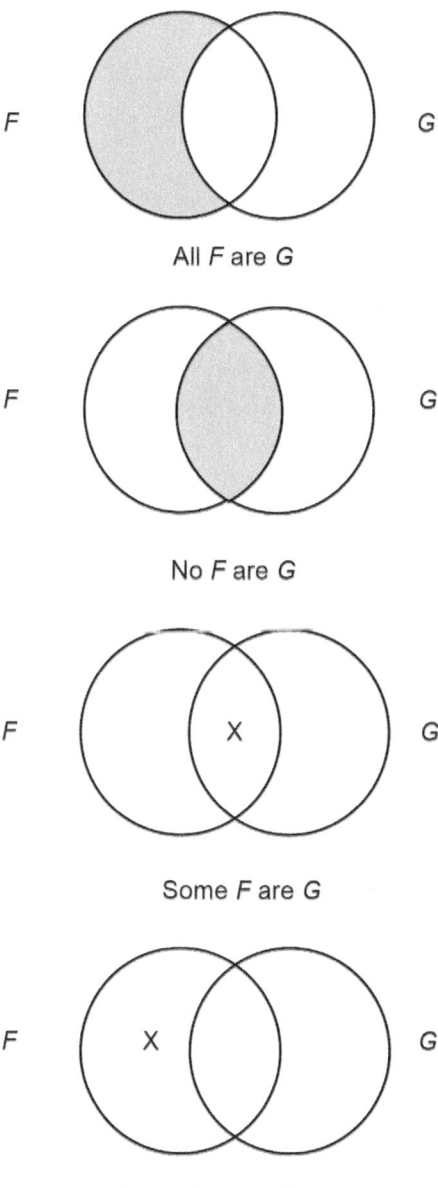

It is important to note that the absence of any marking in a region neither implies that it is empty nor that it is not empty. Rather, it tells us that the statement in question does not inform us one way or the other.

These four kinds of categorical statements can be expressed in many ways that are equivalent from a logical point of view. Take a statement of the form "All F are G." Equivalent expressions include:

- Every F is G
- If anything is F, then it is G
- Nothing is F unless it is G

Similarly, "No F are G" has among its equivalents:

- Nothing is both F and G
- If something is F, then it isn't G
- No G are F

Again, some equivalents of "Some F are G" include:

- There are F that are G
- Some Fs G
- Some G are F

Finally, counterparts to "Some F are not G" include:

- There are F that are not G
- Not all F are G
- Some Fs do not G

It is best at the beginning for students to work with categorical statements in their standard form, which includes giving students practice in recognizing their variants and rewriting them in standard form. Students may also need to be convinced that "No G are F" is logically equivalent to "No F are G" and that "Some G are F" is equivalent to "Some F are G." The best way to do this is to refer back to the diagrams. The diagram for "No F are G" is the same as one for "No G are F" and there is no difference between a diagram for "Some G are F" and one for "Some F are G." This shows their logical equivalence.

We can now proceed to the categorical syllogism. It is an argument that involves two premises and three terms. By introducing a third overlapping circle to represent the categories belonging to the three terms, we can represent both premises in a single diagram. Consider the following syllogistic argument:

Some pitters are snipers.
All snipers are creatures that like to biff.
Therefore: Some pitters are creatures that like to biff.

We can represent the premises on a Venn diagram as follows, employing the letters *P*, *S*, and *B* respectively for *pitters*, *snipers*, and *creatures that like to biff*. We shade all regions of the *S* circle that lie outside of the *B* circle for "All snipers are creatures that like to biff" and place an *X* in the intersection of the *P* and *S* circles for "Some pitters are snipers." It will have to go in the non-shaded region of the intersection, of course, because we know that the shaded region is empty.

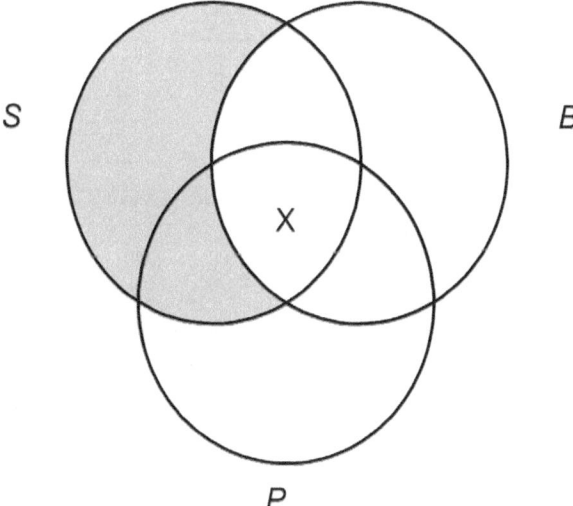

Having conjointly represented the premises, we now look to see whether the conclusion follows from them. If it does, then the conclusion will already be represented on the diagram. In this case, the existence of an *X* in the intersection of the *P* and *B* circles shows us that it is. The fact that the premises give us sufficient information to deduce the conclusion from the diagram without further ado means that the argument is valid. It is impossible for the premises to be true while the conclusion is false.

Let us try another argument using a Venn diagram labeled *M*, *W*, and *D* for *muddy mites*, *worry wops*, and *doodlers* to represent its terms:

No muddy mites are worry wops.
No doodlers are worry wops.
Therefore: No muddy mites are doodlers.

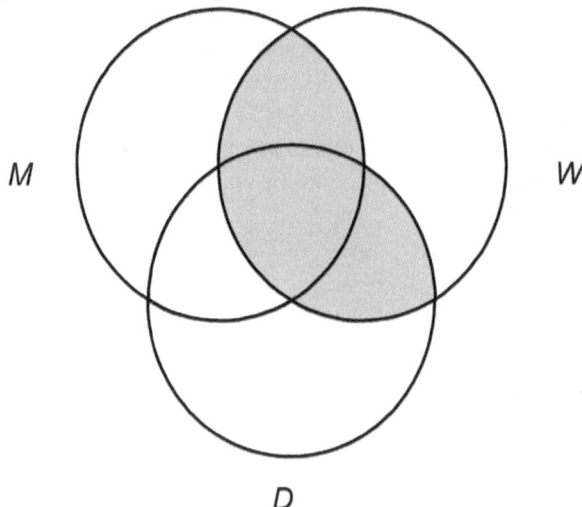

We shade the intersection of the *M* and *W* circles to represent "No muddy mites are worry wops." Then we shade the intersection of the D and W circles to represent "No doodlers are worry wops." Part of that intersection is already shaded, of course, but that's consistent with what we are doing. Both premises tell us that the region is empty. The real problem arises when we look for the conclusion. While one part of the intersection of the *M* and *D* circles is empty, the other part is unmarked. We don't know whether or not it is empty, as the conclusion requires. This means that we can't deduce the conclusion from the premises and the argument is invalid.

One further point needs to be made about the placement of an *X* on a Venn diagram in testing for validity. Sometimes it isn't clear in which part of the intersection of two circles we should place the *X*. Usually we can sort this out if we represent any premise beginning with "All" or "No" first. Otherwise, we should place the *X* on the dividing line so as not to commit us to one part or the other. Having done so, we need to be careful not to draw more information from the diagram than it allows. Consider the Venn diagram for following argument:

Some plants are noxious things.
Some noxious things are deadly.
Therefore: Some plants are deadly.

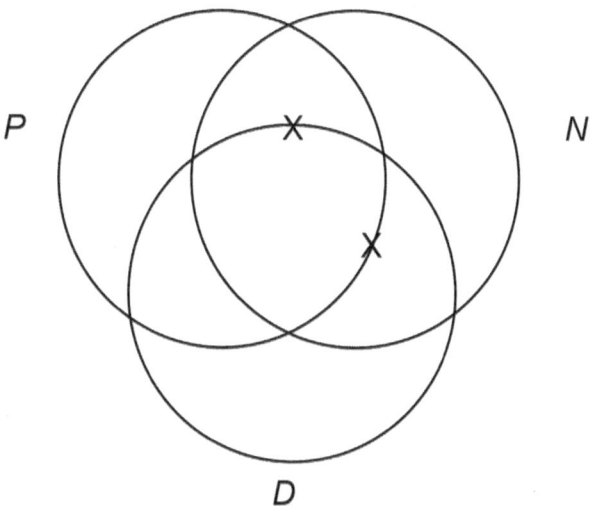

In both cases, the X should be on the line that bisects the intersection of the relevant circles. Consequently, the premises don't tell whether there is anything in the intersection of the *P* and *D* circles. For all we know from the diagram, the things that X denote may lie in the other parts of their respective intersections. The argument is therefore invalid. Although both its premises and conclusion are true, the conclusion doesn't follow from the premises.

Logic texts and sources on the Internet provide copious examples of both valid and invalid categorical syllogistic arguments which can be used to give students practice in working with reasoning of that form. Even so, very little experience is needed to devise them for yourself. That has the advantage of employing content that is appropriate to your setting.

Conditional Forms of Deductive Reasoning

There are two basic forms of valid deductive reasoning that make use of conditionals. To make it clear that we are dealing with the form of an argument, let us use letters in place of statements and also replace "therefore" with a line under the premises to indicate the inference to the conclusion. These forms were recognized in the ancient world and still go by their Latin names.[3]

Modus Ponens

If P, then Q

P

―――――――

Q

Modus Tollens

If P, then Q

Not Q

―――――――

Not P

It can be proved that *modus ponens* and *modus tollens* are valid forms by showing that, regardless of whether the statements substituted for P and Q are true or false, there is no possible combination in which the premises could be true and the conclusion false. Proving this is an elementary undergraduate exercise, but we can dispense with that here. It will be sufficient to rely upon logical intuition to tell us that arguments of these two forms are valid.

These two forms of valid reasoning have invalid counterparts. To say that they are *invalid* is simply to acknowledge that the truth of the premises is no guarantee of the truth of the conclusion in these forms of arguments. They are therefore known as *formal fallacies*. Just as the valid forms involve either affirming the antecedent or if-bit, or else denying the consequent or then-bit, their fallacious counterparts involve either denying the if-bit or else affirming the then-bit.

Fallacy of Denying the Antecedent

If P, then Q

Not P

―――――――

Not Q

Fallacy of Affirming the Consequent

If P, then Q

Q

―――――――

P

Like their syllogistic counterparts, these four forms of argument are so elementary and well known that exercises for them can be found in almost any textbook on reasoning or by a quick search on the Internet. A couple of samples have been constructed below for illustration. The first exercise is meant to be carried out in pairs and does not presuppose the logical notion of validity or prior teaching of the four forms we have discussed. The second is a pen-and-paper exercise for older and more advanced students.

Exercise: Does It Follow?

Work with a partner to answer the following questions: Which of the following examples of reasoning are correct and which are mistaken? Where they are mistaken, can you explain why?

1.
If it looks like a duck, swims like a duck, and quacks like a duck, then it probably is a duck.
It looks like a duck, swims like a duck, and quacks like a duck.
Therefore: It probably is a duck.

2.
If you snooze, then you lose.
You do not snooze.
Therefore: You do not lose.

3.
If it is worth doing, then it is worth doing well.
It isn't worth doing well.
Therefore: It isn't worth doing.

4.
If it is too good to be true, then it probably isn't true.
It probably isn't true.
Therefore: It is too good to be true.

Exercise: What Is Their Reasoning?

When people present arguments, they do not necessarily begin with their premises and end with their conclusion. They may begin with their conclusion, omit part of their reasoning, or leave you to draw the conclusion. Set out the reasoning employed by each of the following four people, beginning with their premises and ending with their conclusion. Having done that, in each case say whether the argument is valid or not.

Becky: Do you know the story about Flight 19 in the Bermuda Triangle? It simply vanished. It means that it was downed by supernatural forces—because that's just what would happen if supernatural forces were at play.

Justine: That's not right, Becky. The area is known for cyclones. If there are cyclones in the area, they can make planes come down.

Tom: I don't think there can be life on Mars. If there were free-flowing water, there could be life. But all the water on Mars is frozen.

Jake: I read a story about biologists who are studying how microbes survive deep in the Antarctic permafrost. If microbes needed free-flowing water, then they couldn't survive under such conditions. But they can.

INDUCTIVE REASONING

In inductive reasoning, the premises do not logically entail the conclusion, but offer merely some reason to suppose that it's true. This kind of reasoning occurs in science.[4] Accumulated evidence may suggest a regularity, which we formulate by way of a generalization, for example, or we might arrive at a hypothesis about the phenomena under investigation by analogy with other cases. The evidence does not logically entail the generalization nor the analogy prove that our hypothesis is correct, but they give us reason enough to suggest them.

In science, these inferences are tentative and subject to further investigation. For example, if our generalization is true, then it should apply in a range of other cases. Here are some other cases. Are they consistent with it? Again, we might devise an experiment for which our hypothesis entails that we should obtain certain results. Let's run the experiment and see what happens.

When things do not turn out as predicted, our reasoning takes a deductive turn and we rely on *modus tollens*: If our conjectures were true, then we would have obtained the predicted results. The results did not turn out as predicted. Therefore, our conjecture is not true—at least, not as it stands, or provided that there is no other credible reason for the failure of our predictions.

Logically speaking, scientific theories and generalizations retain their conjectural status, no matter how well they have been confirmed by experiment and observation. The support provided for them by the evidence never amounts to a logical guarantee, no matter how certain those conjectures may become. From a deductive point of view, therefore, such inductive inferences always exceed the evidence and are in its terms illegitimate. That only goes to show, however, that scientific knowledge is not a matter of logical certainty.

Unwarranted Inductive Inferences

While reasoning from evidence may provide anything from quite minimal support to a practical certainty, unwarranted inductive inferences are ones in which the conclusion clearly exceeds the warrant provided by the premises. We often refer to this as jumping to conclusions. People sometimes jump to conclusions on the basis of very little or otherwise unreliable evidence. This includes overgeneralization by inferring from one or two cases that things are always or generally like that.

When it comes to the classroom, the most common redress is to have students examine the strength of their evidence. What this involves varies from one context to another, of course, but all efforts in that direction will help to combat the all too common habit of rushing to judgment. As regards unwarranted generalization, which is a particular version of this problem, it can be counteracted by encouraging students be on the lookout for possible counterexamples. Here are a couple of illustrations for use with junior secondary students.

Discussion Plan: Jumping to Conclusions

In the following cases, people are basing their conclusions on very little evidence. Have the class discuss what evidence would be needed to say that they were no longer jumping to conclusions.

1. Betty said that she would come around to my place on the weekend, but she didn't turn up—and she didn't answer when I called her on my cell phone. I guess that she's decided not to be my friend any more.
2. People say that the world's climate is getting hotter. Well, last winter was one of the coldest ones in years. So, that ain't right.
3. My uncle says that most people in Boston are wealthier than people in New York. He should know because he's just moved from New York to Boston.

Exercise: Unwarranted Generalization

Provide a counterexample for each of the generalizations below. A counterexample is an example that runs counter to the generalization.

1. An astronomical body orbiting a star is a planet.
2. Mammals are land-based warm-blooded creatures.
3. Lakes are bodies of fresh water surrounded by land.
4. There are 365 days in a year.
5. Birds are creatures that can fly.

Reasoning by Analogy

The fact that states of affairs are like one another in certain respects may give us reason to suppose that they are alike in other respects as well. Suppose that fragments of an unknown ancient hominid are discovered which bear some resemblance to other early hominid species of which we have a more complete record. This gives us reason to suppose that the newfound hominid will resemble them in other respects as well. We might be wrong about that, but it is a reasonable inductive inference.

Let us examine the form of this argument. We will call the new hominid finds $H2$ and the existing hominid record $H1$. Suppose we find that $H2$ shares features x, y, and z with $H1$. In addition, however, $H1$ also has certain other features p, q, and r, for which we currently have no $H2$ record. On the basis of analogy, we infer that $H2$ is also likely to exhibit features p, q, and r.

Sometimes it is said that arguments by analogy involve both an inductive and a deductive step. Let us see what this comes to by reworking our example. From the fact that all previous early hominid finds with features x, y, and z display features p, q, and r as well, we infer that *all* early hominids with features x, y, and z will have features p, q, and r. That is the inductive step. Notice that the conclusion is a universal generalization and goes beyond anything formulated in the original version. From this generalization, together with the fact that the newly discovered hominid has features x, y, and z, we deduce that it will also have features p, q, and r.

Regardless of whether such generalizations are logically required, it can be useful to spell them out. Suppose someone said that thinking is like gardening. You can't do it effectively without appropriate tools. If there is an implicit generalization here, it is the claim that effective work requires the appropriate tools. Spelling this out enables us to scrutinize the argument by looking for counterexamples. It might be said, for instance, that detectives can do effective work without the use of tools—and that thinking is more like detective work than gardening.

Exercise: Arguing by Analogy

The students below have arrived at conclusions about Dan, who is new to the school. In each case, they rely on a general claim that they don't actually state. Taking the cases one at a time, spell out the claim as clearly as you can and discuss whether it is sufficiently plausible to carry the argument.

Noah: Dan is a sporty type, like some other kids in my class. Those kids aren't good at science and things like that. I'll bet that Dan isn't good at them either.

James: All the kids I know who are good at basketball are really tall. Dan isn't very tall. So, he won't be good at basketball.

Emma: Dan's dad dropped him off in a new Cadillac. How many people do you know who own a Cadillac but aren't really wealthy? His dad must be loaded.

Inference from Observation

Inferring things from what you can observe is an indispensable form of inductive inference in everything from scientific inquiry to detective work. Think about detectives investigating a crime scene. The scene may contain many clues as to what happened and who was involved. Detectives look for these clues and draw inferences from them. Sometimes they can do so with great confidence, but on other occasions they may be left to hazard a guess.

The same is true of many other kinds of examinations, as when doctors form a diagnosis on the basis of symptoms exhibited by a patient, astronomers scan images of the heavens for telltale signs of astronomical bodies, and connoisseurs guess the provenance of a wine by examining its color, aroma, and taste. In a less studied fashion, we all do the same in a countless variety of everyday circumstances. Inference from observation is everywhere to be found.

In all such cases, observation involves drawing upon experience and background knowledge. Without that, the observer hardly knows what to look for, or even what they are looking at. It also involves skill. A skillful observer will pick up on things that a less skillful one will miss.

The fact that proficiency in so many fields involves the skillful application of knowledge has educational implications. While application without knowledge is blind, knowledge without application is a mere educational artifact. Hence, we need to provide students with the opportunity to apply their knowledge and to develop skill in doing so in any subject in which observation plays a significant role.

Activity: Inference from Observation in Geography

1. Collect a set of photographs of landscapes related to material that you have been teaching. Set aside one image to display to the class and make up a worksheet displaying the rest of the photos with a set of questions to be answered for each. While questions will vary with the content, they should invite students to make inferences from what they observe, as in the following:
    - What can you tell from the photograph about the climate of the terrain in this picture?

- What can you tell from the photograph about the kind of soils or rocks found here?
- Is there any evidence in the picture to suggest how these structures were formed?

2. Display your set-aside image and engage the class in a brief discussion using the appropriate questions.
3. Divide the class into small groups and distribute the worksheet. Ask the groups to engage in discussion as they fill out the worksheet. Go around the class to encourage inference-making.
4. Choose one group to report their responses to a photo and have the rest of the class ask questions and raise further possible inferences for consideration.
5. Select other groups and do the same for the other photographs.

Reasoning about Causes

We normally rely on inductive inference from the available evidence to figure out what is causing something to occur. In trying to limit the range of possible causes, we may look for a factor or factors that present themselves whenever it occurs. In other words, we look for a common factor or factors across a range of circumstances. We may also look for a factor that is present when the thing in question occurs, but absent when it fails to occur. That is to say, we look for a difference in what are otherwise similar conditions. These two practices, known as the methods of *agreement* and *difference*, are commonly used together.

Sometimes we can have great confidence in inferences warranted by these methods. This is especially so when the patterns we are looking for turn up consistently, or we can manipulate the relevant factors and observe the difference. Even so, it is always possible that unknown factors are in play, so that conclusions derived on this basis never amount to a logical certainty. This is, once again, to acknowledge that the inferences involved are inductive rather than deductive.

While the concept of a cause and the extent of its applicability may be open to dispute, the kind of thinking involved has application across the curriculum. Conditions that constantly precede a certain effect can suggest that they are causal factors in science, just as engrained character traits may be used to explain repeated patterns of behavior in literature. Again, changes in conditions can help to explain the course of historical events in much the same way as they explain them in biology.

Here is an introductory exercise for junior secondary students in which they need to use the methods of agreement and difference to work out what is causing something. Rather than assuming the methods have been taught beforehand, it asks students to figure out the problem and explain how they did so in their own terms. They should be able to get the idea of the two movements in thought with appropriate questioning and guidance from the teacher, allowing a formal introduction to the methods of agreement and difference by way of summing up.

Exercise: Thinking about Causes

Together with your partner, work out what is causing Boofhead to feel ill. You may be called upon to explain your answer to the class. So, besides coming up with your answer, you need to be able to say how you figured it out.

- On Monday Boofhead drank a bottle of Fizzy Pop and ate a packet of Fatty Chips. Later that day he felt ill.
- On Wednesday Boofhead drank a bottle of Fizzy Pop, but decided not to eat a packet of Fatty Chips. On that day he didn't feel ill.
- On Friday Boofhead decided not to drink a bottle of Fizzy Pop, but he did have a packet of Fatty Chips. Later that day he felt ill.

It is worth recalling that inductive arguments as to causes can be converted into deductive ones on the assumption that the causal relation involved invariably holds in that condition. Let us suppose that a Category 2 hurricane is approaching the coast and authorities infer that there will be extensive coastal damage. This judgment is based on past experience of hurricanes with those windspeeds and is a practical certainty. That's not the same as a logical certainty. The fact that hurricanes of this category have always resulted in extensive damage in the past does not *logically* guarantee that they will do so this time. So far, the inference is inductive.

Let us now assume that we are dealing with an invariant causal relation and see how that changes the character of the logical inference.

If a Category 2 hurricane crosses the coast, then there will be extensive coastal damage.
A Category 2 hurricane is crossing the coast.
Therefore: There will be extensive coastal damage.

The prediction is now presented as an outcome of a valid deductive argument. It logically guarantees the truth of its conclusion on the assumption that its premises are true. In particular, it assumes that the conditional first premise has the status of an invariant causal law. It is certainly our best hypothesis based on past experience and we would be foolish not to be guided by it. Even so, were the costal damage not to occur when the hurricane crossed the coast on this occasion, it would show that our major premise is not invariably true.

Inductive reasoning about causes can also rely on concurrent variation, where variation in one thing is accompanied by corresponding change in another. As you increase the pressure on the accelerator, the car increases its speed. As atmospheric pressure falls, so does the level of a mercury barometer. Concurrent variations can have an inverse relationship, where increases in one thing are associated with decreases in another. As global temperatures rise, ice sheets and glaciers retreat. As obesity in a population rises, average life expectancy falls.[5]

NECESSARY AND SUFFICIENT CONDITIONS

Reasoning in terms of necessary and sufficient conditions can be useful in examining both causal and conceptual relationships. To continue with causal relations first, let us say that the cause of something is the condition that is *sufficient*, in the circumstances, to bring it about. This is not to deny that, on another occasion, something else might produce the same result, so that, while the condition in question is sufficient for that effect, it might not be *necessary*. Notice also that we say "in the circumstances" because other background conditions may be necessary for the cause to produce its effect, and we might be interested in identifying them.

There are obviously four possible combinations when it comes to necessary and sufficient conditions between two things X and Y. X can be both necessary and sufficient for Y. X can be necessary but not sufficient for Y. X can be sufficient for but not necessary for Y. X can be neither necessary nor sufficient for Y. These four combinations give us a way of thinking about causal relations, as in the following exercise for junior secondary science.

Exercise: Checking for Necessary and Sufficient Conditions

In the following cases, is X necessary for Y, sufficient for Y, both necessary and sufficient for Y, or neither necessary nor sufficient for Y? Be prepared to give your reasoning.

1. X: clouds Y: rain
2. X: contracting measles Y: having spots on your skin
3. X: sunlight Y: photosynthesis
4. X: being male Y: going bald
5. X: cause Y: effect

Necessary and sufficient conditions are also related in the following manner: If X is necessary for Y and nothing else is necessary for Y, then X is both necessary and sufficient for *Y*. If *X* is necessary for *Y* but other things are also necessary for *Y*, then *X* is necessary but not sufficient for *Y*. If *X* is sufficient for *Y* and nothing else is sufficient for *Y*, then *X* is both necessary and sufficient for *Y*. If *X* is sufficient for *Y* but other things are also sufficient for *Y*, then *X* is sufficient but not necessary for *Y*. (It is possible, of course, that *X* is neither necessary nor sufficient for *Y*, in which case they have no relationship to one another in these terms.)

Causally necessary and sufficient conditions should be distinguished from *logically* necessary and sufficient ones. The presence of clouds may be causally necessary for rain, but it isn't logically necessary in the way that having three angles is necessary for being a triangle. Being deprived of oxygen is sufficient to eventually cause a person to die, but it isn't logically sufficient, as with dying being a sufficient condition for being mortal.

As these examples bring out, logically necessary and sufficient conditions provide a way of thinking about conceptual relationships. Consider apples and fruit, for instance. Being an apple is sufficient for being a piece of fruit. If something is an apple, then it is a piece of fruit. Being an apple is not necessary for being a piece of fruit, of course. If something is a piece of fruit, then it is not necessarily an apple. The following exercise involves reasoning about logically necessary and sufficient conditions for "life" in secondary science.

Exercise: Necessary and Sufficient Conditions

Various criteria are suggested below for being alive. Together with your partner, work out where they belong in the boxes provided, backing up your decision with a counterexample where that is appropriate. For example, if you can think of something that is self-moving but isn't alive, then that would show being self-moving isn't sufficient for being alive.

Criteria: self-moving, grows, breeds, breathes, metabolizes

Neither necessary nor sufficient	Sufficient but not necessary
Necessary but not sufficient	Both necessary and sufficient

CONTRADICTION AND LOGICAL IMPOSSIBILITY

A contradiction asserts or implies something that it also denies. It either is or implies a statement of the form *Both P and not P*. Suppose someone stated that a triangle in plane geometry can have four sides. Since, by definition, a triangle is a three-sided figure and to be four-sided implies not being three-sided, we end up with something being said to be both three-sided and not three-sided, which is a contradiction.

Something is logically impossible if the assertion of it results in a contradiction. It is no more logically possible for a triangle to be a four-sided figure than for a parent to be childless. A "childless parent" is a contradiction in terms—someone who both has one or more children and does not have them. That is not just biologically impossible, but logically impossible.

Exercise: Logical Impossibility

Is time travel logically possible or not? In order to think about this, see whether the following time-travel scenarios involve contradictions. To show that a statement involves a contradiction, you need to demonstrate that it both asserts and denies the same thing.

- You travel in a time machine back to a time before you were born.
- As a result of a postnuclear disaster, a robotic Terminator is built and sent back in time and prevents the disaster from happening.

ANALYZING AND EVALUATING REASONING

Once students are familiar with indicator words for premises and conclusions and have a general idea of the forms of argument, then they are ready to begin to analyze argumentative passages. Since arguments are not always presented in a standard form, with the premises successively laid out prior to a conclusion being drawn, there is all the more need to take a methodical approach to analysis. The recommended procedure runs as follows:

1. Begin by ascertaining whether the passage contains reasoning leading to a conclusion. If so, the presence of argumentative structure and indicator words should enable you to identify the conclusion. Write out or copy and paste it and mark it as a conclusion using the letter *C*. (Be aware that

passages may contain more than one argument and that the conclusion of one argument may be used as a premise for another.)
2. Identify the reason or reasons given in support of the conclusion. Premise indicator words should provide some guidance. As you may need to disentangle premises from one another, be sure to scrutinize any complex-looking reason to see whether it contains more than one claim. Also, be on the lookout for hidden premises. These are premises that aren't explicitly stated, but are needed for the argument.
3. Write out or copy and paste the premises, each one on its own line above the conclusion, labeling them in order as *P1*, *P2*, *P3*, and so on. If you need to reword some of the premises in the process, be careful to avoid any alteration in meaning. Where there are hidden premises, don't forget to include them. You can indicate that they are hidden by putting *H* in brackets at the end of the line. Preserve the order of your premises, if that is clear from the passage. Otherwise, put them in the order that makes best sense of the argument.

Having analyzed the argument, it is ready for evaluation. There are two tasks here, one having to do with the acceptability of the premises and the other with the inference to the conclusion. It might be that the premises imply the conclusion, but one or more of the premises is dubious or false, thus weakening or nullifying the argument. Conversely, the premises may be true, but the inference is faulty, either because the argument is formally invalid or because the inductive connection is weak or even nonexistent. For the argument to go through, it must succeed on both counts.

If the argument is deductive, then it is said to be *sound* if, and only if, its premises are true and the argument form is valid. Logic cannot guarantee the truth of the premises, of course, and other steps may need to be taken in order to verify them. So far as the validity is concerned, you should at this point stick to material that involves only the four basic forms that were introduced earlier.

If the argument is inductive, then it will succeed only to the extent that its premises are well grounded and provide sufficient evidence for the conclusion. What constitutes sufficient evidence is as much a practical as a logical matter, but students at the secondary level should be made aware that the strength of inductive arguments sometimes can be judged with a fair degree of mathematical precision. Statistical findings in many fields are effectively the conclusions of inductive arguments. Such findings are based on evidence that may imply a conclusion within a mathematically well-defined range of probability.

Chapter 4

MAPPING ARGUMENTS IN DISCUSSION

While students need to be introduced to reasoning through instruction and exercises, we are ultimately concerned with its use in collaborative inquiry. This includes reasoning in class discussion as well as reasoning in pairs and small groups. We will begin with class discussion, where the teacher has the best opportunity to request, model, and guide reasoning moves in the flow of inquiry.

So far, we have concentrated on drawing conclusions from premises. Reasoning in inquiry-based class discussion, in contrast, commonly takes the form of logical justification, in which reasons are provided in support of a suggestion. When students make a suggestion during class discussion, it is generally appropriate for the teacher to ask them to support it with reasons. We may call these reasons *justifications* for the suggestion and represent their relationship as shown.

At this point, other students may supply further justifications of the suggestion, or they may say why they disagree with it or with the support given to it. Let us refer to the reasons that mark any disagreement here as *objections* and add them to our schema.

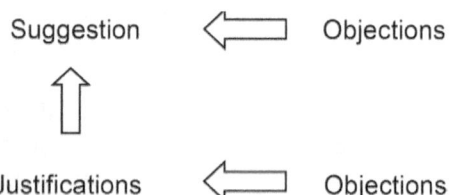

It is important to note that, while objections to justifications may bring the truth or reliability of justifications into question, they may also provide reason to doubt the inferential support claimed for the suggestion. We could mark this distinction by introducing a further arrow pointing back to the one between the justification and the suggestion, but it is simpler to note the basis of the objection in the way that you write it up.

Objections, in turn, may bring forth *replies* that run counter to the objections in one way or another. Once we have added them to the schema, we have all the basic building blocks for recording argumentative discourse in collaborative inquiry. While we could consider objections to the replies and so on, these are just further iterations of the moves already represented.

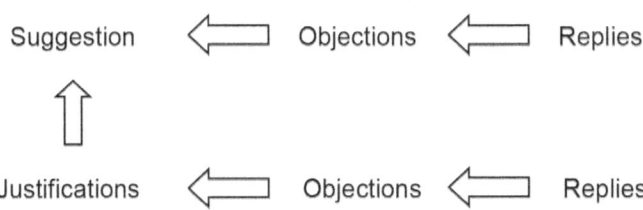

It would be time-consuming and cumbersome to record all the reasoning that occurs about suggestions in the course of inquiry-based class discussion. Even so, much is to be gained by using this schema to record extended episodes of reasoning on the board. It helps the students to keep track of those deliberations and promotes greater depth of understanding about the most important suggestions.

Don't forget that reasoning is a two-way process that proceeds by logical justification in one direction and by inference in the other. We constructed our schema by following the normal flow of deliberative discussion. If we read the schema in the direction in which the arrows flow, however, the arrows represent inferences in which we have:

- justifications as premises with the suggestion as conclusion,
- objections as premises that lead to the denial of the suggestion as conclusion,
- objections as premises that lead to the denial of one or more justifications as conclusion, and
- replies as premises that lead to the denial of one or more objections as conclusion.

Students should be aware of the inverse relationship between justification and inference from their introduction to reasoning. Still, it is worth underlining this point when working on the board with the reasoning schema by encouraging students to work in the direction of inference as well as of justification.

Here is a short verbal exchange involving argumentative give-and-take. It is somewhat artificial and meant only as an illustration of the reasoning schema, the terms of which have been italicized.

Teacher: Our question is whether we should morally judge people's actions by their consequences. Does anyone have a *suggestion*?

Stephen: I reckon that we should judge what people do by the consequences of their actions.

Teacher: Can you provide some *justification* for that *suggestion*, Stephen?

Stephen: Well, what people do can cause harm, or good can come of it too, and that's what matters in the end.

Beth: I have an *objection* to what Stephen is saying. You might do something that happens to benefit others, but do it just for your own selfish reasons. That's doing something for the wrong kind of reason. It has nothing to do with what happened as a result.

Teacher: Stephen, would you like to *reply* to Beth?

Stephen: I agree with Beth that it isn't good to be selfish. So, I guess that we ought to take people's motives into account. But whether or not you do something for your own selfish reasons, the consequences still matter.

The teacher's use of the italicized words is deliberate. It signals the moves that students are being asked to make. It may seem a little heavy-handed, but it is not a bad idea to encourage students to use that language too. In that way, they become clear about what move they are making and signal it to others. If this bit of discussion were sufficiently important to track on the board, it would go roughly as shown.

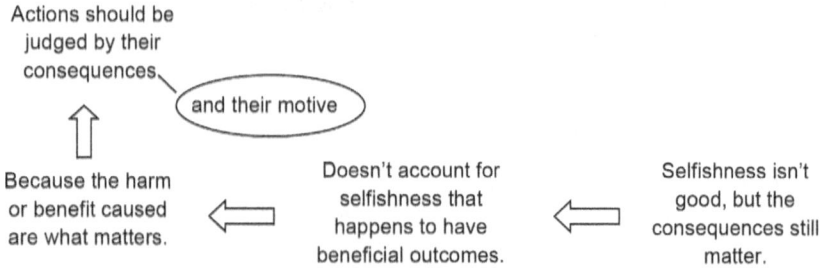

As discussion moves along, further justifications, objections, and replies may be given. As a result, suggestions might be modified—as we see here—or even abandoned. This is not to overlook work on competing suggestions and their connections with other reasoning on the board. Extensive discussion, particularly of complicated problems and issues, increases the need for judicious recording, so as not to end up with a board so cluttered with argumentative detail as to be more of a hindrance than a help. The use of bullet points that capture essential points can help, as can keeping the discussion focused rather than allowing it to become diffuse.

Something to notice about the snippet of dialogue above is the teacher's use of procedural questioning to elicit the requisite moves in reasoning as the discussion proceeds. As elsewhere in guiding class discussion, the use of questions to elicit appropriate moves in students' thinking is central to the teacher's role. Typical questions to help generate justificatory and critical reasoning moves include:

Eliciting justification

- What is your reason for thinking that's true?
- Can you back that up?
- Can anyone think of another reason to support that suggestion?
- Is that sufficient reason, or do we need some further justification here?

Eliciting objections

- Are there any objections?
- Does anyone disagree with that?
- What might someone say if they disagreed?
- Does anyone have any other concerns about what's being claimed here?

Eliciting replies

- Do you have a reply to that?
- What might someone say in reply?
- Is there a response we could make to that challenge?
- Do you think that objection works?

Once you have modeled this way of working with the class using the reasoning schema and students are sufficiently familiar with it to use it independently, you can build it into small group work. When students need to address a proposition by reasoning about it, you can divide the class into groups, give each group a large sheet of paper and marking pen and set them to work. You can do the same thing with a question, problem, or issue, about which there are only two or three viable options, so that the students end up reasoning about a manageable number of competing suggestions.

The following activity presumes that the teacher has introduced the class to reasoning maps in the way outlined above and that they are ready to begin group work using the reasoning schema. While the students are given a set of instructions to follow, they may still need a helping hand. This means that the teacher should keep a close eye on things and move between the groups to ask questions and issue reminders. The activity could form part of project work, be a preliminary exercise for argumentative essay writing, or simply lead to one or two groups presenting their results and fielding questions within the same lesson.

Group Activity: Argument Mapping

1. Starting with your question at the top of your sheet, come up with a couple of suggestions that your group thinks are the best possible answers to it and write them down.
2. What is the main justification for each suggestion? Add them to your sheet using a dot-point or a simple sentence to start building a reasoning map.
3. Can you think of any serious objections to the suggestions, or to the justifications you have given for them? Add them to your map.
4. Can you think of any replies that might be made to these objections? If so, add them to your map.
5. Having considered the matter, what conclusion would you be inclined to draw? Write that conclusion below your map, together with any qualifications relating to unresolved issues.

The mention of essay writing is a reminder that, among other things, we are aiming to cultivate good reasoning in written and other individual work. As with collaborative inquiry-based learning in general, we are working toward this in three stages:

1. The explicit teaching of reasoning accompanied by the kinds of exercises to be found in this chapter.
2. Students reasoning in pairs or in small groups with no more than intermittent teacher support.
3. Individual students having sufficiently internalized reasoning operations to be able to carry them out on their own.

EXERCISES AND ACTIVITIES

The Language of Reasoning

Many words can operate as reasoning indicators. In addition to our starter words "because" and "therefore," other words pressed into service in the exercises below include "since," "as," "for," "so," "consequently," "given that," and "it follows that."

Exercise: Giving a Reason

Underline the word that shows the people below are about to give a reason.

Emma: My cousin is annoyed with me because I forgot her birthday.
Liam: Since I was away all last week, I have a lot of catching up to do.
Mason: You will need to talk louder as I cannot hear you.
Harper: Because you told a lie, I got into trouble.
Lucas: My sister has to go to bed earlier than I do, for she is much younger than me.

Exercise: Drawing a Conclusion

Underline the word or words that show the people below are about to draw a conclusion.

Ben: I didn't do it. So, you shouldn't blame me.
Charlotte: 3 times 8 is 24 and therefore 8 times 3 is also 24.
Michael: Since a square has one more side than a triangle, it follows that it has one more angle as well.
Sophia: Dogs are more friendly than cats and consequently they make better pets.
Evelyn: Given that he has always been late in the past, he will probably be late again.

Exercise: Words That Show Reasoning

Sometimes the word "so" is used to say that something follows and at other times it is not used that way. Circle the word "so" in the passage below where it is used to show that something follows.

> The winter had been so mild that the ice on the lake was thin. So, the hunter knew that it was dangerous to go out there. Still, he trudged on so as not to be thought afraid. "It can handle the weight of a bear," he said to himself, "so it can take the weight of a man." It was only when the ice around him began to crack that he realized it was not so.

Exercise: Words That Indicate Reasoning

Underline the words which indicate that a reason is about to be given or a conclusion drawn in the following passage:

The witness insists that she met the defendant for the first time on the morning of the crime. We know that isn't true because she was seen with him in Minneapolis on the previous day. So, she is lying. It follows that she has something to hide. If she were his accomplice, then she would obviously try to conceal that fact. Therefore, we need to question her further about the reasons for her trip to Minneapolis.

Justification and Inference

As was pointed out earlier in this chapter, reason-giving includes both explanation and justification. Both cases come in more than one variety. There are causal explanations and personal explanations. There is moral justification and logical justification. Reasoning is particularly concerned with the last of these, but with young students you might find it easier to start with causal explanation to get the practice of reason-giving going.

Warm-up Activity: Reason-giving with "Because"

Here is the procedure to follow:

1. After setting up your discussion circle, choose a student to complete a sentence, such as "The boy fell off his bicycle *because* . . ." by giving a reason why it happened—for example, "He fell because he slipped."
2. The next student is to attempt to complete a "because" sentence by building on the first child's contribution—in the example, by saying, for instance, "He slipped because the path was icy."
3. Continue on around the circle until you desire to call a halt, allowing children to pass if they have difficulty. (If two children in a row cannot answer, allow anyone in the class to answer, and then continue from where you left off.)

Once you have established the use of "because" and "therefore" as basic reasoning indicators, it is time to get them working together and for students to come to appreciate the inverse relationship between justification and inference.

Exercise: Because and Therefore

We use the word "because" to give a reason and the word "therefore" to say that something follows from what was said. Use these two words to fill in the blanks in the following story:
Andy was afraid _____ there was a ghost in his bedroom. _____, he ran downstairs to tell his mother. Andy's mother didn't believe in ghosts.

_____, she smiled and took Andy back upstairs. She told the ghost to show itself, _____ she said the ghost would get into trouble if it did not do as it was told. That must have frightened the ghost _____ it popped out of the wardrobe. It was Andy's sister Sandy, being a tease.

Exercise: Giving Reasons and Drawing Conclusions

In the following cases, say whether Biff and Miff are giving a reason or drawing a conclusion. If they are offering a reason, turn around what they have said into drawing a conclusion. Similarly, if they are drawing a conclusion, turn around what they have said and make it into giving a reason.

Biff: There is no such thing as an ideal dog because no dog is perfect.
Miff: Given that dog shows judge actual dogs against the ideal, it follows that there must be an ideal dog.
Biff: There is no such thing as a perfect circle because not one of the things we regard as a circle is perfectly circular.
Miff: There must be such a thing as a perfect circle because we use it to judge that something like a wheel isn't perfectly circular. (Be sure to fill out what "it" means when you reverse what Miff is saying.)

We also need to give students practice in drawing conclusions by way of logical inference from a set of premises. That can also be an occasion to have them also present the arguments in the reverse direction, starting with the conclusion and justifying it by citing the premises using "because."

Exercise: Giving Reasons and Drawing Conclusions

What conclusion can you draw in the following cases? Write it down. Be ready to justify your conclusions by citing the two premises using "because."

1. Some teachers are philosophers. All philosophers are a little mad. *Therefore:*	2. All saws are cutting tools. All cutting tools need sharpening. *Therefore:*
3. All bats are nocturnal. No nocturnal animals have color vision. *Therefore:*	4. All movie stars are famous. Some actors are not famous. *Therefore:*

Conditional Reasoning

The following activities and exercises illustrate some ways in which you can make use of conditional reasoning for successively older age groups.

Activity: An "If... then" Round

This activity proceeds by taking the consequent (the then-bit) of a conditional statement to be the antecedent (the if-bit) of a second conditional statement and so on.

Here is the procedure to follow:

1. Remind the class about sentences of the "If ... then ..." kind, using the expressions "if-bit" and "then-bit," if you like.
2. Give the class an "if" clause to be completed with a "then" clause (e.g., "If I could fly like Superman . . ."). Choose a student to complete the sentence, beginning with the if-bit.
3. Ask the next student around the circle to use the "then" clause contained in the first student's response as their "if" clause to construct a new "If ... then ..." statement. (Let us suppose, for example, that the first student said, "If I could fly like Superman, then I would become a superhero." The next student would start with "If I became a superhero, then . . ." and complete that sentence.)
4. Continue following the same procedure until you have been right around the circle or run out of time. If a student has difficulty completing a statement, ask whether someone can help by suggesting a response. Then go back to the student who was being helped and have them use that prompt.

Exercise: An "If... then" Story

Turn the bits and pieces below into a story. Each sentence in the story must be made from two bits, with an *if* before the first bit and a *then* to join it to the second bit.

The pirates had a treasure   it is where there is a skull and cross bones on the map
I keep digging beneath all these bones   I am sure to find it   I might not feel so dizzy
they must have hidden it on the island   I have read the map correctly   this is the spot
the sun stopped beating down on me   I had something that I could eat or drink
I might have the strength to go on digging   the treasure is buried on the island

Activity: If... then

This activity can be conducted with students in pairs using a long strip of paper, a piece of tape and a marking pen.

Reasoning

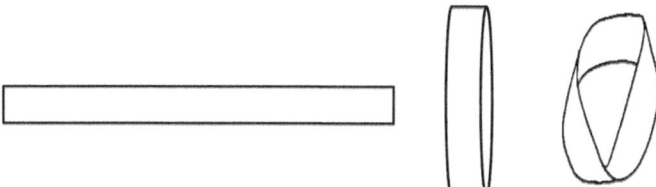

1. Beginning with the whole class, have students answer the following two questions. As you do so, have students try to define the terms "edge" and "surface." Keep a tally of the number of edges and surfaces on the board.
   - If you have a rectangle, then how many sides and surfaces does it have?
   - If you join the ends to make a cylinder, then how many sides and surfaces does it have?
2. Now have students answer the question below by (1) having the class generate alternative hypotheses, (2) having the class devise a way of testing their hypotheses, and (3) having students carry out the test in pairs. Then add the results to the board.
   - If you twist one end of the paper by 180° and join the ends, how many sides and surfaces do you have?

The following is a warm-up exercise in secondary science in preparation for the introduction of the Newtonian formula for calculating gravity. It asks students to make inferences based on their existing knowledge. There is likely to be disagreement or uncertainty when it comes to the final question, however, which can afterward be resolved by applying the formula to the supposition about the moon and the earth.

Warm-up Exercise: Gravity

1. If you increase the angle at which you fire cannonballs into the sky, then . . .
2. If there is no air resistance and you drop objects of different weights from a height, then . . . .
3. If you let go of an object in the space station, then . . . .
4. If you bounced a basketball while on the moon, then . . . .
5. If the moon were as massive as the earth, then . . . .

Deductive Reasoning

When it comes to deductive reasoning, it is important for students to appreciate that, given a set of premises, the conclusion follows with logical certainty, so long as you don't make mistakes in your reasoning.

Exercise: What Must Follow?

Given some things, others must follow. What must follow given the things below?

1. Fido is a dog and all dogs like bones.
2. It only snows in the winter and we have snow.
3. Abby is taller than Bobby and Bobby is taller than Candy.
4. All fires are hot and all hot things can burn you.
5. If you gulp your food down, then you get the hiccups, and you do not have the hiccups.

Exercise: Drawing Conclusions

See how many conclusions you can draw from the following statements and any combination of them.

Nathanial is older than Rachel.
Rachel is older than Nicky.
Nicky is younger than Max.
Max is younger than Sam.
Sam is older than Nathanial.

Activity: Therefore

1. Divide the class into pairs and give each pair a sheet with the statements as set out below.
2. In each of the four sets of statements, one of them can be concluded from the other two using "therefore." Give the students a few minutes to decide in each case which of the three statements is the conclusion.
3. Check out the results with the class and have them discuss any conflicts or mistakes that may have arisen.

1.
No squirrels make good pets.
No wild animals make good pets.
All squirrels are wild animals.

2.
All creatures that sleep through the winter can store up fat.
Ground squirrels sleep through the winter.
Ground squirrels can store up fat.

3.
Some squirrels do not live in a burrow.
Some squirrels can glide through the air.
Nothing that can glide through the air lives in a burrow.

4.
Groundhogs are good at forecasting the weather.
Some squirrels are good at forecasting the weather.
A groundhog is a kind of squirrel.

Here is a rerun of the arguments above set out formally. Students may find it more challenging, so it should be used as a follow-up to the previous activity.

1.

No □ are O.

No ✿ are O.

All □ are ✿.

2.

All ♦ are ☙.

ℂ are ♦.

ℂ are ☙.

3.

Some □ are not Ψ

Some □ are Ө.

No Ө are Ψ.

4.

All ⓜ are ☼.

Some □ are ☼.

A ⓜ is a kind of □.

Exercise: Checking for Validity

Check the following arguments for validity using Venn diagrams.

1.
No horned animal is a carnivore.
All moose are horned animals.
Therefore: No moose is a carnivore.

2.
All supporters of the United Nations policy want to preserve peace.
None of the countries that the president has condemned support the United Nations policy.
Therefore: None of the countries that the president has condemned want to preserve peace.

3.
All birds are feathered creatures.
All birds are creatures capable of flight.
Therefore: All creatures capable of flight are feathered creatures.

Exercise: Valid or Invalid?

Using Venn diagrams, work with a partner to determine which of the following arguments are valid and which of them are invalid.

1.
Some sailors are bound to get seasick.
All those bound to get seasick are best to stay on land.
Therefore: Some sailors are best to stay on land.

2.
Some seaworthy boats are naval vessels.
Some naval vessels are state of the art.
Therefore: Some seaworthy boats are state of the art.

3.
No worthy sea captains are the first to desert a sinking ship.
Some who are the first to desert a sinking ship are cowards.
No worthy sea captains are cowards.

4.
All sailors in the navy are entitled to shore leave.
All those entitled to shore leave are returning from service at sea.
Therefore: All sailors in the navy are returning from service at sea.

This chapter introduced two elementary valid forms of deductive reasoning involving conditions and contrasted them with their invalid counterparts. By the time students enter secondary education, students should be able to distinguish between these forms of valid and invalid reasoning.

Exercise: Mistakes in Reasoning

Which of the following forms of reasoning are valid and which are invalid? Where they are invalid, can you explain why?

1.
If there is a red sky tonight, then tomorrow will be a shepherd's delight.
There is a red sky tonight.
Therefore: Tomorrow will be a shepherd's delight.
2.
If you eat an apple a day, then you will keep the doctor away.
You do not eat an apple a day.
Therefore: You will not keep the doctor away.
3.
If it is good for the goose, then it is good for the gander.
It is good for the gander.
Therefore: It is good for the goose.
4.
If people were meant to fly, then they would be born with wings.
People are not born with wings.
Therefore: People were not meant to fly.

Exercise: Mistakes in Reasoning

Which of the following forms of reasoning are valid and which are invalid? Where they are invalid, can you explain why?

1.
If you are a zombie, then you eat human flesh.
You do not eat human flesh.
Therefore: You are not a zombie.
2.
If Bigfoot exists, then there should be giant footsteps in the snow.
There are giant footsteps in the snow.
Therefore: Bigfoot exists.
3.
If King Kong can climb the Empire State Building, then he can climb all the buildings in the world.
King Kong cannot climb all the buildings in the world.

Therefore: King Kong cannot climb the Empire State Building.

4.
If he is put in charge of Monsters Inc., then Monsters Inc. will harvest children's laughs instead of their screams.
He is put in charge of Monsters Inc.
Therefore: Monsters Inc. will harvest children's laughs instead of their screams.

Another strategy for showing that someone's reasoning has gone astray is to supply a *counterexample*—that is, an example of an argument of the same form in which the premises are true but the conclusion is obviously false. Just because Elle has buckteeth and rabbits have buckteeth, it doesn't follow that Elle must be a rabbit, as is argued in the exercise below. To show this, you need only replace Elle with something else that has buckteeth. Beavers would do. You might as well say that beavers have buckteeth, rabbits have buckteeth, and therefore that beavers are rabbits—which obviously they aren't.

Exercise: You Might as Well Say

Some of the following examples of reasoning are mistaken. Can you spot them? Where the reasoning is mistaken, replace one of the premises with a different example to show that it is mistaken.

1.	2.
Elle has buckteeth.	This is a foot long.
Rabbits have buckteeth.	Twelve inches is a foot long.
Therefore: Elle must be a rabbit.	*Therefore:* This is twelve inches long.
3.	4.
Santa has a long white beard.	We have a small dog.
The man in red has a long white beard	A Pomeranian is a small dog.
Therefore: The man in red is Santa.	*Therefore:* We have a Pomeranian.
5.	6.
The earth is a sphere.	Nathan won the last race.
A planet is a sphere.	A new kid won the last race.
Therefore: The earth is a planet.	*Therefore:* Nathan is a new kid.

Finally, people sometimes arrive at conclusions on the basis of false or dubious assumptions. Assumptions act as supporting premises which often are merely implicit in our reasoning. They need to be called to account when they may be false or dubious.

Exercise: Making Assumptions

In the following cases, people are reaching conclusions based on questionable assumptions. Try to identify those assumptions in discussion with a partner.

1. Zoe insisted that Greenland is larger than America. She saw Greenland on a world map and it was larger in size.
2. Emma claimed that Chicago could not be badly damaged in an earthquake because it isn't on a fault line, like San Francisco.
3. Mason was sure that the sun went around the earth every day. After all, it rose in the east every morning, made its way across the sky, and set in the west.
4. Benjamin says that a lump of gold is bound to weigh the same on the moon as on Earth because it is just the same amount of gold that is being weighed.

Inductive Reasoning

We need to guard students against unwarranted inductive inference which all too easily can become an ingrained habit. Jumping to conclusions on the basis of insufficient evidence and the related tendency to overgeneralize, together with relying on unrepresentative samples or dubious authorities, are the main culprits here.

Discussion Plan: Jumping to Conclusions

In the following cases, people are reaching conclusions without much evidence. Have the class discuss what kinds of evidence would be sufficient to say that they are no longer jumping to conclusions.

1. Jamie must have been the one who broke the classroom window because he's always getting into trouble.
2. I'll bet your dog has fleas. Mine does.
3. Most kids want me to be class captain. I've asked a few and they said they'll vote for me.
4. My dad takes me fishing, but the last couple of times we didn't catch much. It looks like the fish are disappearing from the lake.

Discussion Plan: Unwarranted Generalization

In the following cases, people are drawing a general conclusion that is not justified by the evidence. Have the class discuss what makes the evidence insufficient and what kind of evidence would be required to draw such a conclusion.

1. Everyone in my family has always been heavy. We're all healthy. So, there's nothing wrong with being heavy when it comes to your health.
2. I have seen a report by a scientist saying that there is no such a thing as manmade climate change. So, scientists don't really believe in it.
3. There are no boys in the book club that I belong to. It shows that boys don't read books.
4. I read about a volcano that erupted in Indonesia in 1883 that killed more than 36,000 people. It sure is dangerous to live near a volcano.

One way of having students avoid an uncritical acceptance of generalizations is to encourage them to be on the lookout for counterexamples. Here are a couple of more challenging exercises involving the search for counterexamples to generalizations, one relating to mathematics and the other to spelling.

Exercise: Unwarranted Generalization

Provide a counterexample for each of the generalizations below. A counterexample is an example that runs counter to the generalization.

1. The sum of two numbers is always greater than either of them.
2. The product of two numbers is always greater than either of them.
3. All prime numbers are odd numbers.
4. If p is an odd number and is prime, then $p+2$ is also a prime number.

Exercise: Provide a Counterexample

A counterexample is an example that runs counter to a general rule. Try to come up with one or more counterexamples to the following grammatical rules.

1. When you join two words into one, keep all the letters (e.g., *play* and *mate* becomes *playmate*).
2. When a word ends with an *e*, do not drop the *e* when adding a suffix that starts with a consonant (e.g., *sincere* becomes *sincerely*).
3. When a word ends in *e*, drop the *e* when adding a suffix that begins with a vowel (e.g., *dare* becomes *daring*).

4. If a word ends with a *y* preceded by a vowel, then keep the *y* when adding a suffix (e.g., *play* becomes *played*).
5. If a word ends with a *y* preceded by a consonant, then change the *y* to *i* when adding a suffix (e.g., *fry* becomes *fried*).

Exercise: Biased Samples and Misplaced Authority

Sometimes people reach conclusions from an unrepresentative or biased sample of evidence. At other times, they draw conclusions by relying on some misplaced reference to authority. These errors occur below. Can you identify where they occur?

1. The students at this school want more money spent on sports facilities. I took a survey of the kids in the baseball team and they all said so.
2. Glenda Glamorous, the movie star, recommends Crowning Glory Shampoo. It must be really good.
3. Did you notice that yesterday's weather forecast turned out to be wrong? There are other occasions that stick in my mind when the same thing happened. It shows that weather forecasting is pretty much hit-and-miss.
4. Americans need to lose weight. Nearly all the leaders of business and industry think so.
5. Horoscopes really can predict the future. Twice now someone has picked the winner of the Grand National by consulting their horoscope.

Let's now turn to analogical reasoning. Don't forget that in dealing with analogical reasoning it is sometimes useful to identify the underlying generalization that is being relied upon and look for counterexamples.

Discussion Plan: It's because They Are Similar

Have the class discuss whether the reasons given by the people below are good ones, ensuring that they listen carefully to one another and engage in the give-and-take of reasons.

Mitch: You shouldn't be upset when you see a cat playing with a mouse. It's as natural for a cat to play with a mouse as for a dog to play with a ball—and you wouldn't be upset by that!

Ella: It is mothers who have the babies, not the fathers. That's why it is only natural for girls to have dolls, but not boys.

Tilly: You have to join in with whatever happens at a birthday party. Otherwise it's like going to someone's place for dinner and refusing to eat the meal.

Exercise: Arguments Based on Analogies

In the following arguments a consequence is drawn from a comparison between two things. How plausible are the arguments?

1. Water is essential to life on earth, but scientists have also found water on Mars. So, there is likely to be life there.
2. You shouldn't blame social media for the rise in online bullying. It's like blaming motorcars for a rise in road rage.
3. Both coffee and cigarettes are stimulants, but we don't restrict the advertising of coffee. So why should we restrict the advertising of cigarettes?

Exercise: Arguing by Analogy

Evaluate the following arguments. How good are the analogies they involve? Are the similarities sufficient to make the arguments good ones, or are there differences that undermine them?

1. You cannot promote peace in the world through war. It is like trying to foster good relations with your neighbors by having a nasty argument with them.
2. Sap is like blood in bringing nutrients to where they are needed. Therefore, just as there is a circulatory system for the blood in an animal, there will be one for sap in trees.
3. A well-ordered society requires intelligent rulers who make good regulations that the citizens obey. Similarly, we can say that to be a well-adjusted person you need to use your intelligence to make good decisions and then stick to them.

Let's turn our attention now to inference from observation. There are obviously plenty of opportunities to make inferences from observations in teaching science, but it can also be introduced into other parts of the curriculum. Here are three examples, the first an activity for the later elementary school years, the next a secondary school exercise in science, and the third a stimulus for a creative writing assignment.

Activity: What Happened Here?

For this you will need access to a sandy area. Wet sand on a beach is best, but a sand pit is fine if you moisten the sand and rake it smooth. Before bringing the class to the spot, have a couple of students enact a simple scene that will leave its imprint on the sand. Then have the students gather around and make suggestions as to what happened and discuss them.

Exercise: Inference from Observation

Use a photograph with telltale signs to get students thinking about what they are observing. A photograph of star trails, for instance, suggests both the rotation of the earth and the direction of its axis. If you can tell what hemisphere the photograph was taken in, you can also pick true north. (While it might initially be argued that the circular pattern of star trails suggests only relative rotary motion, to interpret the stars as moving in that pattern relative to one another depends on untenable assumptions, as students should be able to work out.) Simply display the image to the class and have students make suggestions and try to justify them, or divide the class into small groups to see what inferences they can make on the basis of what evidence.

Writing Assignment: Murder Mystery

1. Collect a series of visual clues to a fictitious crime. Scan them and place them in an electronic file which you can print or send to students. The clues should be such that, by inference from careful observation, a variety of coherent narratives can be told about what happened and who was involved.
2. Have the students write a short story based on inferences that they can make from the clues. They can construct the narrative as they like, so long as it makes use of all the material provided and draws reasonable inferences from it.

We come now to reasoning about causes.

Exercise: What's the Explanation?

On the basis of the information given, what's the most likely explanation of the following things?

1. Last year the weather was unusually hot and dry during the growing season and, despite adding extra fertilizer, the crops did not do well. Although we had good rain this year, the temperatures were up again. After the disappointing result last year, we couldn't afford additional fertilizer this year, but nonetheless we had good crops. I guess you've figured out what made the difference.
2. Texacola looks and tastes just like Mexicola, but Texacola sells much better. Both companies spend a fortune on advertising, although Texacola presents itself as being all-American, while Mexicola has a south-of-the-border image. Of course, lots of other soda pops also make a big play of being American but nothing sells like Texacola. How come Mexicola doesn't do so well?

3. It's a curious thing that kids who are good at math are often good at music. As it turns out, nearly all of them have been studying music since they were little. Not everyone who is good at math is musical, of course, and there are kids who are good at music but not good at math. That last group has also been studying music for years. I'm not sure what all that says.
4. Over the past few years, new movies have been released for home consumption rather than for the big screen. For many years people have been saying that movie theatres are going to be a thing of the past. Once it was because of television. Then it was because of things like Netflix. But somehow movie theatres survived. Yet, for some reason they have recently gone into steep decline.

The following exercise provides an opportunity to combine the methods of agreement and difference. As students work on it, it is important for them to come to see that both procedures are required to home in on the likely cause.

Exercise: Reasoning about Causes

Work with a partner to figure out what caused the downturns in Universal Corporation's share price and be ready to explain your reasoning.

- Three years ago, Universal Corporation posted a large profit. The company paid a handsome dividend to the shareholders and its executives received huge bonuses. Its share price went up.
- Two years ago, Universal Corporation posted a large profit. It paid its executives large bonuses, but put most of its profit back into the company. Its share price went down.
- Last year, Universal Corporation made a loss. While the company cut executive bonuses, after last years' experience, it decided to pay a substantial dividend to shareholders. It's share price went up.
- This year, Universal Corporation once again made a loss. It cut executive bonuses once again and decided to put most of its money back into the company. Its share price went down.

Before engaging students in the following exercise, you need to explain to them how inductive reasoning about the cause of something can be turned into a deductive argument by assuming that the cause and effect in question fall under a causal generalization or law. If we believe that the cause of Y is X, then the standard form for such an argument is:

If X, then Y.
X
Therefore: Y

You will find an example in the section on reasoning about causes earlier in the chapter. It can be used for illustration, unless you prefer to make up an example of your own.

Exercise: Construct a Valid Argument

Construct a deductively valid argument based on the reasons given as to why these things occurred.

1. A wildfire in northern California is thought to have been caused by lightning strikes following a long period of dry weather.
2. Two lightly dressed mountaineers froze to death after unexpectedly being snowed in for several days on Mont Blanc in the French Alps. Unfortunately, it was only to be expected, as the temperature remained well below freezing over that period.
3. Fish stocks in the seas around China have fallen dramatically. Analysts blame years of heavy government subsidies handed out to local fishermen to keep up with the demand for fish.

Finally, we come to necessary and sufficient conditions.

Exercise: Necessary and Sufficient Conditions

In thinking about causes, and their effects are the conditions listed under C necessary, sufficient, or both necessary and sufficient for those listed under E?

C	E
1. Balanced diet	Good health
2. Showering	Getting wet
3. Heat increase	Rise in temperature
4. Serious injury	Pain
5. Power failure	Lights going off
6. Fires	Smoke

Exercise: Causally and Logically Necessary Conditions

The conditions listed under A are necessary for those listed under B. Which of them are causally necessary and which of them are logically necessary?

	A	B
1.	Power supply	Electrical lighting
2.	Having four sides	Being square
3.	Water	Growth of plants
4.	Cold weather	Snow
5.	Being male	Becoming an uncle
6.	Being colored	Being red

Exercise: Necessary and Sufficient Conditions

Taking the pairs in the table in the order in which the two things are presented, work out which of the four conditions applies. Be ready to explain your reasoning.

	Necessary but not sufficient	Sufficient but not necessary	Both necessary and sufficient	Neither necessary nor sufficient
Circling a star/ being a planet				
Being a planet/ circling a star				
Being a natural satellite/being a moon				
Belonging to a constellation/ being near one another in space				

Contradiction and Logical Impossibility

Exercise: Are You Contradicting Me?

Some of the people below are contradicting one another, while others are not. Can you pick them?

1.
James: All the countries in South America speak Spanish.
Michael: They speak Portuguese in Brazil.
2.
Emma: I reckon that every planet in the solar system has an atmosphere.
Mia: At least the earth does.
3.
Ronald: Some kids are not happy about the test coming up on Friday.
Kevin: No one is happy about it.
4.
Isabella: Some of the guys in this class are hot.
Charlotte: None of them are.

Exercise: Paradoxes

The following scenarios involve a paradox in that they look as if they lead to a contradiction. In each case, try to answer the question at the end and see if you can uncover the contradiction.

1. In Sicily long ago there was an old man who was a barber. The tyrant who ruled Sicily at that time commanded him to shave all and only those men who do not shave themselves. Could he do so?
2. On a river bank in India a crocodile snatched a baby. The baby's mother pleaded with the crocodile to give her baby back. The crocodile agreed to give the baby back if she could correctly answer a simple question, but otherwise he would eat her baby. The crocodile's question was simply this: Will I eat your baby or will I give it back? Can the mother succeed in getting her baby back?
3. In the gloomy depths of winter in Russia, a weary traveler came to a bridge where everyone who passes must state their business. If they answer truly, they are allowed to pass. But if their answer proves not to be true, then they are executed on the spot. The traveler stated his business as follows: I have come to be executed on this spot. What happened then, I do not know. Do you?

Analyzing and Evaluating Reasoning

A search of local newspapers or articles on the web can easily turn up argumentative passages for your students to analyze and evaluate. Three passages suggested by newspaper reports are set out below, one with a single argument and the other two with conflicting arguments. Analysis of the latter could be used as a warm-up for discussion.

Exercise: Set Out the Argument

Identify the conclusion and the premises of the argument presented it in the passage below. Then set out the argument.

> *An Australian court heard today that the winning entry of the Archibald Prize for portraiture should be disqualified. It was argued that the portrait mainly used charcoal rather than paint and in technique had all the hallmarks of a drawing rather than a painting. This put it in breach of the rules for the Archibald Prize, which stated that it must be awarded to "the best portrait painting."*

Warm-up Exercise: Set Out the Arguments

Together with a partner, set out the arguments to be found in the passage below. What do you think of them? Be prepared for discussion.

Japan has recommenced whaling. While conservationists argue that many species of whales were hunted almost to extinction, proponents point out that the minke whale, which Japanese whalers mainly hunt, is not on the endangered list. Even so, many who oppose whaling point out that whales are a highly intelligent species, raising welfare as well as environmental concerns. Japanese whalers also complain that foreigners need to show some respect, as whaling is part of Japanese culture and people from different cultures ought not to be criticizing longstanding Japanese traditions.

Warm-up Exercise: Set Out the Arguments

Together with a partner, set out the arguments to be found in the passage below. What do you think of them? Be prepared for discussion.

A local pastor has expressed grave concern that a Swedish crematorium has started heating homes with the energy from burning bodies. He said that the practice shows a lack of respect for the deceased as well as their loved ones. A representative of the crematorium responded by saying that it means that the crematorium is no longer releasing excess heat and poisonous gasses into the environment, thereby contributing to a cleaner environment. He added that it has also helped to keep down the energy costs of the crematorium.

NOTES

1. We speak of *logical* justification in order to distinguish it from the justification of behavior. When our actions are called into question, we may attempt to justify them by giving reasons for what we did. Logical justification, however, deals with relations between statements.

2. Eric Carle, *The Very Hungry Caterpillar* (New York: World Publishing Company, 1969).

3. *Modus ponens* is the affirmative mode in which we affirm the antecedent or if-bit of the conditional, whereas *modus tollens* is the negative mode in which we deny the consequent or then-bit of the conditional.

4. The claim that scientific reasoning is largely inductive has been the subject of controversy in the philosophy of science. This is not the place to enter into the debate; it will be sufficient for our purposes to acknowledge that deductive reasoning plays an important role in scientific testing, irrespective of the role of induction.

5. Reasoning from concomitant variations often takes the form of statistical arguments, but that takes us into specifically mathematical considerations which are beyond the scope of this book.

Bibliography

Cam, Philip. "Philosophy for Children." *Oxford Bibliographies*, in "Philosophy." Edited by Duncan Pritchard. New York: Oxford University Press, 2018. https://www.oxfordbibliographies.com/page/philosophy.

Cam, Philip. *Teaching Ethics in Schools: A New Approach to Moral Education*. Melbourne: ACER Press, 2012.

Cam, Philip. *Twenty Thinking Tools: Collaborative Inquiry for the Classroom*. Melbourne: ACER Press, 2006.

Carle, Eric. *The Very Hungry Caterpillar*. New York: World Publishing Company, 1969.

Dewey, John. *Democracy and Education*. New York: Free Press, 1966.

Dewey, John. *How We Think. Buffalo*. New York: Prometheus Books, 1991.

Dewey, John. *Logic: The Theory of Inquiry*. New York: Henry Holt and Company, 1938.

Einstein, Albert. *Relativity: The Special and the General Theory*. New York: Bonanza Books, 1961.

Fisher, Robert. *Teaching Children to Think*. Hemel Hempstead, Herts: Simon & Schuster, 1990.

Fisher, Robert. *Teaching Thinking: Philosophical Enquiry in the Classroom*, 3rd edition. New York: Continuum, 2008.

Goering, Sara, Nicholas J. Shudak, and Thomas Wartenberg, eds. *Philosophy in Schools: An Introduction for Philosophers as Teachers*. New York: Routledge, 2013.

Gregory, Maughn, Joanna Haynes, and Karin Murris, eds. *The Routledge International Handbook of Philosophy for Children*. New York: Routledge, 2016.

Hannam, Patricia, and Eugenio Echeverria. *Philosophy with Teenagers*. New York: Continuum, 2009.

Haynes, Joanna. *Children as Philosophers*. New York: RoutledgeFalmer, 2002.

Lewis, Lizzy, and Nick Chandley, eds. *Philosophy for Children Through the Secondary Curriculum*. London: Continuum, 2012.

Lipman, Matthew, Ann Margaret Sharp, and Frederick S. Oscanyan. *Philosophy in the Classroom*, 2nd edition. Philadelphia: Temple University Press, 1980.

Lipman, Matthew. *Philosophy Goes to School*. Philadelphia: Temple University Press, 1988.

Lipman, Matthew. *Thinking in Education*. New York: Cambridge University Press, 1991.

Lone, Jana Mohr, and Roberta Israeloff, eds. *Philosophy and Education: Introducing Philosophy to Young People*. Newcastle upon Tyne: Cambridge Scholars Publishing, 2012.

Luria, Alexander Romanovich, and F Ia. Yudovich. *Speech and the Development of Mental Processes in the Child*. Harmondsworth, Middlesex: Penguin Education, 1959.

Luria, Alexander Romanovich. *Cognitive Development: Its Cultural and Social Foundations*. Translated by Martin Lopez-Morillas and Lynn Solotaroff. Cambridge, MA: Harvard University Press, 1976.

McCall, Catherine. *Transforming Thinking*. New York: Routledge, 2009.

Nozick, Robert. *Anarchy, State and Utopia*. New York: Basic Books, 1974.

Paul, Richard. *Critical Thinking*, 3rd edition. Cheltenham, Vic: Hawker Brownlow, 1993.

Piaget, Jean. *Genetic Epistemology*. Translated by Eleanor Duckworth. New York: Columbia University Press, 1970.

Piaget, Jean. *Judgment and Reasoning in the Child*. Translated by Marjorie Warden. New York: Harcourt, Brace and Co., 1928.

Piaget, Jean. *The Child's Conception of the World*. Translated by Joan and Andrew Tomlinson. Lanham, MD: Rowman & Littlefield, 1951.

Piaget, Jean. *The Language and Thought of the Child*, 3rd edition. Translated by Marjorie and Ruth Gabain. New York: Routledge, 2002.

Pritchard, Michael S. *Reasonable Children*. Lawrence: University Press of Kansas, 1996.

Salmon, Wesley C. *Logic*, 3rd edition. Englewood Cliffs, NJ: Prentice-Hall, 1984.

Shapiro, David. *Plato Was Wrong!: Footnotes on Doing Philosophy with Young People*. New York: Rowman & Littlefield, 2012.

Vygotsky, Lev Semenovich. *Mind in Society: The Development of Higher Psychological Processes*. Edited by Michael Cole, Vera John-Steiner, Sylvia Scribner, and Ellen Souberman. Cambridge, MA: Harvard University Press, 1978.

Vygotsky, Lev Semenovich. *Thought and Language*. Edited and translated by Eugenia Hanfmann and Gertrude Vakar. Cambridge, MA: MIT Press, 1962.

Wartenberg, Thomas E. *Big Ideas for Little Kids*. Lanham, MD: Rowman & Littlefield, 2009.

Wilson, John. *Thinking with Concepts*. London: Cambridge University Press, 1971.

About the Author

Dr Philip Cam is Honorary Associate Professor in the School of Humanities and Languages at the University of New South Wales, in Sydney, Australia. He has a DPhil in Philosophy from the University of Oxford and is an international authority on philosophy in schools. He has run workshops for educators in many countries and, aside from his academic publications, has written numerous books for teachers and children, which have been widely translated. His books include *Thinking Together*, *Twenty Thinking Tools*, and *Teaching Ethics in Schools*, as well as philosophical stories published as the *Thinking Stories* series of storybooks, *Sophia's Question,* a philosophical novella, and *Philosophy Park*, a history of philosophy in story form.

www.ingramcontent.com/pod-product-compliance
Lightning Source LLC
Chambersburg PA
CBHW022014300426
44117CB00005B/184